Tips, Tricks And $ Advice They Didn't Teach You In College.

Trey Smith,

CFP®, ChFC, CRPC, CIMA

The Tips, Tricks And $ Advice They Didn't Teach You In College.
Copyright © 2009 by Trey Smith

ISBN 978-0-578-15866-2

Printed in USA by 48HrBooks (www.48HrBooks.com)

Dedication

Two separate groups were instrumental in the completion of this book. The first is my family including my wife Dianne and daughters Katelyn and Larissa, because without their love and support the successes I have had would matter very little.

The second group is made up of the twenty-something's that spent time both reviewing the book for errors but also making sure that it was relevant to their demographic. These include (in chronological order of when they reviewed the book) Andrew Mauney, Will Sterling, Crystal Morgan, and Mat Tyndal. Crystal and Mat are a part of my team at SunTrust Investment Services, Inc. in Nashville.

This list of people who have supported could go on almost infinitely – you

Table of Contents

To Risk

To laugh is to risk appearing a fool,

To weep is to risk appearing sentimental

To reach out to another is to risk involvement,

To expose feelings is to risk exposing your true self

To place your ideas and dreams before a crowd is to risk
their loss

To love is to risk not being loved in return,

To hope is to risk despair,

To try is to risk to failure.

But risks must be taken because the greatest hazard in life is
to risk nothing.

The person who risks nothing, does nothing, has nothing is
nothing.

He may avoid suffering and sorrow,

But he cannot learn, feel, change, grow or live.

Chained by his servitude he is a slave who has forfeited all
freedom.

Only a person who risks is free.

The pessimist complains about the wind;

The optimist expects it to change;

And the realist adjusts the sails.

~William Arthur Ward

Preface

Why I wrote this book?

This book is an attempt to offset the damage that the mass media and incompetent advisors have done to my clientele. Since many have children, it's also a primer to get their kids off to a great start in life. Unfortunately most people do not know how to talk to their children about money; it's one of the strongest taboos left in our society.

There is no reason that any young person has to get off to a bad start financially; especially considering the simple techniques that can be used to avoid most financial land-mines. My goal is to help you avoid those mistakes and correct the ones you've already made.

Since this is my first book, please don't expect it to be the smoothest ever written. As a matter of fact, it will be chock full of bad stories and terrible sarcasm. And frankly, I don't care. This is primarily how I speak: simple and straightforward. The only thing I'd do differently is try to customize the information, just for you. Since no book can completely overcome this barrier, please seek help when the time is right.

Why this book?

The biggest differentiator between what you are reading, here, and all of other financial planning books is, quite simply, you the reader. Compare yourself to the average person who picks up a financial book. First ask yourself, "What do they (the typical financial reader) want out of the experience?" Then inquire, "What do I hope to accomplish?" Chances are your goals aren't identical since many financial planning books are written to target a very broad market. Frankly, many of them target anyone who thinks they can get rich overnight. The antithesis of the "get-rich-quick" book isn't a common-sense financial guide; it is a literary version of financial boot camp. It is a little like reading the worst diet/fitness book you can imagine. Reading one of these books feels like they are telling you to run 15 miles, do 50 chin-ups, and 500 crunches. Then, if you are really, really good, you can have a carrot and sugar-free Jell-O for dessert. Once you have completed the Ironman Triathlon. The only difference is that you substitute saving, scrimping, sacrificing for exercising.

The majority of the financial boot-camp books are targeting individuals who have had a hard time just making ends meet on a month-by-month basis. For that reason, they are primarily geared not just to people who earn less than $50,000 per year, but to people who are also in debt because they've been ordering all of the get-rich-quick schemes on late-night television.

Introduction

The challenges facing today's young adults have, arguably, never been greater. Businesses are often extraordinarily competitive now as they frantically struggle to keep pace in the Digital Age and compete in a global marketplace. Workers are faced with the burden of keeping up – or being left behind. Society is transforming along with the economy.

The impact of all of this on our lives is great. We've seen an explosion, and enormous innovation, in apps; we can shop online for most of our necessities now (and find customer reviews for pretty much anything and everything); and investors have never had more resources at their fingertips for making sound investment decisions. At the same time, we seem to have never had *less* time in our days. And scams abound.

As I will mention in Chapter 2, Ryan Johnson, Special Agent to the FBI and annual speaker at my client presentations, explains that cybercrime is quickly becoming the most pervasive type of crime in the United States. He says that "it's estimated that for the FBI, cybercrime will probably be our #1 priority in a few years". Most cases lead overseas, there are approximately 16,000 new viruses manufactured every day and in 2010, identity thieves cost individuals approximately $5 billion and businesses $48 billion nationwide. Ryan tells my clients that although the Internet is a key part of financial management now, all financial transactions should really be done on a separate computer.

"The challenges facing today's young adults have, arguably, never been greater. Businesses are generally extraordinarily competitive now as they frantically struggle to keep pace in the Digital Era and compete in a global marketplace. Workers are faced with the burden of keeping up – or being left behind. Society is transforming along with the economy."

It's important to become educated about the risks while sticking with the fundamentals, so you can focus on building a solid and successful future like your parents and grandparents before you. This is what I am here to show you how to do. The foundation for this is turning down the noise, safeguarding your assets and staying with a lot of tried-and-true principles. As you will see in Chapter One, the key is to learn how to manage your money so that your money doesn't end up managing you. That is what this book is all about.

So let's get started, shall we? Game on!

"It's important to become educated about the risks while sticking with the fundamentals. So you can focus on building a solid and successful future like your parents and grandparents did. And this is what I am here to show you. The foundation for this is turning down the noise, safeguarding your assets and staying with a lot of tried-and-true principles."

Chapter 1

Game On!

When you know a thing, to hold that you know it; and when you do not know a thing, to allow that you do not know it -- this is knowledge.

~Confucius (551 BC -- 479 BC), The Confucian Analects

Imagine this:

You land your dream job right out of school. For you, that may mean the executive track at a Fortune 500, starting a new business, acting on Broadway, or, as in the case of Freddie Scott Jr., playing in the National Football League. Fame and fortune greeted him immediately upon graduating from Penn State in 1996. He became a wide receiver for the Atlanta Falcons, earning a massive six-figure paycheck and following in the footsteps of his dad, Freddie Scott.

"You're living your dream," he told me. "There's nothing like waking up in a hotel and having a police officer escort you to the stadium. Or walking into the locker room and seeing your jersey hanging there with your name on it, and the game-day magazine with your picture, stats and bio. I'll never forget the first time I played in San Francisco's Candlestick Park against Jerry Rice, Steve Young and Ricky Watters, or in Dallas against Troy Aikman, Michael Irvin and Deion Sanders. The year before, I was watching those guys on television."

He tells me that while he's enormously grateful to have gotten off to a good start financially, many NFL players do not. He managed his annual $200,000-plus paychecks frugally by establishing a $5,000-a-month budget, which included his rent. Still, unplanned injuries and personnel changes truncated his career.

Fortunately, he was able to start the next chapter of his life without the burden of debt or student loans, but he still had to make lifestyle changes. He had_to get a nine-to-five job, live frugally, and begin building a brand-new life from scratch. Today, he educates other NFL players on managing that critical transition.

"With the NFL, we try to educate players about the fact that we are an anomaly in that most people earn very little money in their early 20s. Your income generally increases over time, you set a little away and, eventually, you have your nest egg. For professional athletes, you are looking at two to 10 years when you are earning a boatload of money that you are *not* going to earn when your career ends. And so you have to protect that front-loaded income and allow it to work for you. So you don't have to work for money later."

The fact is that the savvier you are at managing your money *today,* the less time you will spend letting money manage you *later.* It's that simple. And there's absolutely no reason why any young person has to get off to a bad start financially, especially considering the simple techniques that can be used to avoid most financial land mines. My goal is to help you avoid those mistakes and correct the ones you've already made while there is still plenty of time.

"The fact is that the savvier you are at managing your money *today,* the less time you will spend letting money manage you *later.* It's that simple."

After all, dreams will come and go. But planning is forever. Scott, for example, told me that he saw his dad's nine-year professional football career end in bankruptcy after a multimillion-dollar contract with the USFL fell apart. Sponsorships and birthday parties on Detroit's Ford Field eventually ended. Life, for all of us, winds up as a series of chapters and transitions. Some will read like a fairy tale; others *will* include reversals of fortune. But money will make it all a whole lot easier and the road worthwhile.

"Dreams will come and go. But planning is forever."

However, this will mean truly investing in your future and I'm here to show you how to do it intelligently.

Now, since this is my first book, please don't expect it to be the smoothest ever written. It reflects how I speak: simple and straightforward. This book is designed for people who know that the only person who ever gets rich from a get-rich-quick scheme is the person who devises it. They understand that financial planning isn't about fighting a war; to the contrary, it's about steadily building a future. So this book will not make you rich tomorrow. But with a little luck, you'll be able to put your own kids through college one day, retire in a lifestyle that will make you proud, and pass on considerable wealth to those you care about.

As Freddie once told me, "Your money will go where your heart is."

So, what's most important to you? What does success for you really look like? From here, you can begin a really cool discovery process.

.

Chapter 2

How to Make Saving a Habit

You have purchased all of the necessities and maybe even a few luxuries, so now it is time to start saving!

Now, you may be thinking that there are one or two more things you need. Or another luxury that a friend has that you don't.

Well, get over it!

If all your friends do is buy things instead of saving for their future, they will be poor their entire lives. Start saving NOW so you won't.

It's that simple.

A dollar saved and invested at 12 percent works out to roughly $3 that you don't have to save in 10 years, $9 dollars that you don't have to save in 20 years, $30 that you do not have to save in 30 years and $90 you will not have to save in 40 years. So start saving now!! No little trinket you buy today will be worth what you will eventually have.

"If all your friends do is buy things instead of saving for their future, they will be poor their entire lives. Start saving NOW so you won't."

To help make saving fun, check out websites like LivingSocial.com, Groupon.com and Restaurant.com for daily discounts on a multitude of things. For travel, I like Orbitz and Priceline. Aggregation apps like Mint and Mvelopes allow for budgeting right from your phone in addition to providing account balances.

Budgeting means nothing more than knowing your exact income and outgo and having a plan for managing your money. It's very difficult to stick to your financial goals without one since you'll be driven more by momentary needs and desires. One of my best friends, William MacDougall, the CFO of Do-All Outdoors in Nashville, has already amassed a $200,000 portfolio, at just 41 years of age, by adhering to a strict budget.

"The key is really just having an understanding of cash flow. My wife, Anna, and I still today go through our cash flow budget every few months; what we currently have, and what we are expecting and forecasting. We are on a strict budget. But we adjust and correct as needed and know exactly where we are every day."

"The key is really just having an understanding of cash flow. My wife, Anna, and I still today go through our cash flow budget every few months; what we currently have, and what we are expecting and forecasting."

They have succeeded entirely through planning and hard work; it's just so incredibly important to have a plan, budget and to start saving on a regular basis – for life. Financial stress ruins relationships and can even cause health problems. These issues cannot be overstated. So getting started on a good path in life is all about your financial wellbeing.

So what's your first step on the path towards prosperity?

Step #1: Keep a healthy cash reserve as your first defense against life's mishaps.

Three months of expenses for many people may seem like a tremendous amount of idle cash, especially when you are living paycheck to paycheck. However, it really is only the starting point of where your reserve should be.

Murphy visits everyone!

We have all heard of Murphy's Law and he visits all of us from time to time. Unfortunately, if you are not ready for the visit, it can go from being an annoyance to a catastrophe. Let's look at the simple example of a broken wrist. I doubt there is a single person who has not seen someone with a cast on their arm, so we all know how common it is. The question is, how would you deal with it if it were to happen to you? A simple injury like this will involve two things. First, it would incur medical bills, and second, for many of us, lost work time.

"Three months of expenses for many people may seem like a tremendous amount of idle cash, especially when you are living paycheck to paycheck. However, it really is only the starting point of where your reserve should be."

What amazes most people is that this can be just as traumatic for a contractor as it is for a surgeon. For both of these individuals, the most likely cause of bankruptcy is disability and it doesn't even have to be a long-term condition. Let's look at the example of someone I worked with who practices rather delicate surgery. Life was (and still is) good for this client. She has a loving family, which includes three kids, two of whom happen to be in college. Sally and her husband were taking a dream ski vacation over the Christmas break with the entire family. Unfortunately, on the second day, she shattered her wrist in a fall.

Because they were out of the country, her health insurance would not pick up the costs of the initial treatment and, due to the severity of the break, she was rushed back to the United

States to have surgery. At this point, this story could have gone one of two ways.

First, let's consider if this accident had happened two years earlier before the client had started working with me. As a couple, they had a combined annual income of well over $500,000, but little savings outside of her 401(k) and the equity they each had in their practices. They were deep in debt and basically living paycheck to paycheck. Both of them had group insurance including disability. However his disability was capped at $7,500; hers, at $5,000; and neither policy started paying for 90 days.

Because of the accident, and the rehab that resulted, she was out of work for approximately six months. By the end of the sixth month, she would have lost $120,000 in income! Disability payments would have made up $15,000. Although $15,000 is better than nothing, it would not have even covered her medical expenses while she was out of the country.

Medical bills and lost income probably would not have pushed this couple into bankruptcy, but by the end of the sixth month they would have been so far behind that it would have looked like a pretty good option. Fortunately for them, they had already started to correct their financial situation. In doing this, they had taken four rather dramatic actions.

First, instead of maxing out their 401(k) contributions, they contributed only up to their employer's maximum matching amount. With the difference in savings, they were able to pay down all of their credit card debt. Second, instead of buying a new car as quickly as they paid off their current car, they put off purchasing a new car for two years and saved what had been their monthly bill for their next car. Third, they both increased their personal disability insurance. And finally, they started investing $100 per month in a money market account as their cash reserve; they then increased the $100 every month until it became noticeable to them. Most people are surprised by just how much they can save by taking this approach.

How has their life changed?

Well, they had gone from $1,563 in monthly debt payments to $427 (they still had one car payment), their cash reserve was up to $14,000, and their disability insurance payments had increased by $9,000 per month for a total increase of $27,000 of tax-free benefits. What a difference it made. Instead of considering bankruptcy, they just stopped saving for the six-month period she was out of work and dipped into their car fund.

Where are they today? They currently have six months in cash reserves (although it is not just sitting in cash), no consumer debt, and are well on their way to retirement. What could have set them back for years barely even slowed them down. If it ever happens again, financially it will barely impact what they are working to achieve.

The most amazing thing is that even with college payments, they have more money to spend and less stress. And anyone can do this.

The important thing is to just get started!! Also, if you don't see it, you won't spend it! So hide it!!

The best place to keep your cash reserve, and any other savings, is as far from your checking account as possible. Humans – well, at least Americans - have a tendency to spend everything that is in their checking accounts. So separate all savings (not just the cash reserve) from your monthly expenditures.

"The best place to keep your cash reserve, and any other savings, is as far from your checking account as possible."

Only move the money when you are making a large and necessary purchase. And then only move the money that you have budgeted for the purchase. It's simple to do a little homework on the web, find what you are looking for, and then just transfer the necessary funds into your checking account: doing this will help you stay within your budget.

A very simple, yet, effective strategy.

The other great benefit is that you can earn additional money on your savings. One simple way to do this is by keeping your first month's reserve in cash and your next two to three months in rolling CDs or even short-term government bonds. For the remaining months, you can try low-risk bond funds and very conservative balanced funds.

This way, you still maintain access when you need it. The majority of your reserve is principle-protected, but you still have an opportunity to get a little growth - especially since you should be in the market for at least a couple of years. Hopefully you will never have an incident that requires you to use all of your cash reserve. But let's say you do in 10 years. At that stage, your earnings should have outpaced a money market return even if the balanced fund has fallen on hard times.

The one thing I must stress is that these are <u>not</u> high-risk dollars. You are looking for investments that carry little or no risk. Make sure that whomever you are working with knows that you may need these dollars at anytime. Smaller fluctuations and easy access are more important than large gains since these are the dollars you use when things go wrong, like losing your job.

Remember a recession can cause both the job market to freeze up and the stock market to decline, so don't take risks with your cash reserve no matter what returns your buddy promises you.

"Remember a recession can cause both the job market to freeze up and the stock market to decline, so don't take risks with your cash reserve ..."

Replacements?

When it is time to make a big purchase, like a car or a new roof, should the money be pulled from cash reserves? The answer is no; your cash reserve is for emergencies and unforeseen events <u>only</u>. You need to save specifically for other big-ticket items because if you do not, then every time your cash reserve hits a certain point, you will go out and purchase a new car, putting your cash reserve back to zero!

Saving for a new car and investing in a cash reserve does not mean you have to have a separate account for both. It just means that you always leave a minimum of six months in your reserves that you cannot dip into unless there is an emergency. Beyond that number, money may be used for planned expenditures like a new car or a down payment on your next home!!

Once you have enough to buy two cars, diversify even further.

Sooner than most people expect, you may have saved enough to cover any big-ticket item within the next five years. If this is the case, it is time to diversify your portfolio into more growth-oriented positions. The important thing to remember is that even if all of these dollars are in the same account, you need to be able to differentiate between investments comprising your cash reserve and investments earmarked for the long term. If you haven't allocated them this way, you are probably taking too much risk or too little.

Retirement Savings – You Aren't Counting on Social Security Are You?

Since you are reading this book, I am just going to assume you are smart enough to know that you cannot depend upon Social Security for all of your needs in retirement. Having said that, I do believe it will still exist in some form, but who knows what it will look like 30 to 40 years from now. For all we know, it may morph into a strict welfare benefit instead of a retirement benefit. For this reason, you must invest.

So let's look at some of the basics.

The two most common approaches to investing are lump sum and dollar-cost averaging*. For many of us, it is a moot point. We really do not have a choice as to which of these approaches we are going to use because of the way we are saving.

*Regular investing does not assure a profit against a loss in declining markets. Dollar Cost Averaging involves continuous investments in securities regardless of fluctuating price levels. Investors should consider their financial ability to continue purchases through periods of low price levels.

"The two most common approaches to investing are lump sum and dollar-cost averaging."

Lump Sum Approach

The name alone tells you that this isn't for everyone. To invest a lump sum, you need the lump. If you do not have tons of cash just sitting around to invest, then you can't be a lump-sum investor.

Some people argue that they are lump-sum investors because they save all year and put money into the market just once a year - at the same time every year. The reality is that they are still dollar-cost averaging, but they are just doing it annually instead of monthly. For some people, this style of investing (which is a hybrid approach between the lump sum and dollar-cost averaging approaches) works well, especially if they are building up a cash-reserve account that they never have to tap into.

One of reasons you may have a lump sum to invest is because you have come into a large windfall of cash. Great Aunt Birdie died, you won the lottery, you got your first big bonus, or Mr. Murphy never came to visit your home so your rainy day fund has grown to the point that it would make Noah proud. The other type of lump-sum investing that I see frequently involves moving funds from a 401(k) to an I.R.A.

Once you have cash beyond your cash reserve (and savings for large purchases), your money needs to go into the stock market for the long haul.

You are better off getting your money into the market sooner rather than later. There are, however, two exceptions to this rule (at least historically). First, the months of summer through early fall have a tendency to be the worst-performing months of the year so you may want to wait until November or December before you drop your nest egg into the market. This is, of course, assuming that you are going to do it all at once.

"You are better off getting your money into the market sooner rather than later."

The other exception is that for many people, spreading the dollars out over six months may allow them to sleep better even if it does not help their returns. One way to identify if you should spread it out over a period of months is what I call the "Buyer's Remorse Index." If, after you purchase something, you never check its price again, then you are probably a good candidate to invest the money all at once. You have a very low occurrence of Buyer's Remorse.

On the other hand, if you continually check the prices on items you have already purchased, you would probably be better off by spreading your investments out over a period of six to 12 months. Chances are that it won't help your return, but it may help you sleep better.

Dollar-Cost Averaging (DCA) Approach

For most people, dollar-cost averaging is the way they must invest for retirement. We invest monthly into 401(k)s, Roth I.R.A.s, and savings accounts because we really have no other choice. Our income comes in monthly, so saving happens monthly as well. Even if you invest an annual bonus or your tax refund, it still counts as dollar-cost averaging. You are just doing it annually instead of monthly.

The reality for the average young investor is that you will probably be putting your dollars into the market as quickly as possible by following the model of monthly investing. If we assume that the market generally increases over time, and that it goes up more often than it goes down, doesn't it make sense to invest in it as quickly as possible? Especially if there is a way to do it and not feel like you are putting your entire nest egg at risk?

Do not believe the hype of buying low and selling high. The reality is that the faster the money goes into the market, the longer it has to grow.

If you wait to do a large investment then you may miss a period of growth in the stock market while you let your cash sit on the sidelines. In other words, the main reason to dollar-cost average is not to try and play the minor month-to-month market fluctuations, but to get the money into the market as fast as possible because the odds are more in your favor every additional day your money is invested.

Dollar-cost averaging is simply the way to *save* so someday you will have large lump sums to invest.

"Do not believe the hype of buying low and selling high. The reality is that the faster the money goes into the market, the longer it has to grow."

Now that you know that you have to dollar-cost average, where do you do it?

Qualified programs

Better known as retirement plans, qualified plans are what the **I.R.S.** and the federal government officially recognize as tax-preferred methods for saving for retirement. Most of these programs also fall under what is called "ERISA."

But frankly, you don't care about any of that.

For the purposes of this book, I am going to simplify this: If your investment has a special tax treatment and you have to tell the I.R.S. how much you put in and take out each year, then it is qualified. Another way to identify something that is probably qualified is if you take money out too soon (before 59 1/2), they will penalize you. Or if you take it out too late (after 70 1/2), they may hit you again. In real terms, anytime you have money in a qualified program, there are strings attached.

"If your investment has a special tax treatment and you have to tell the I.R.S. how much you put in and take out each year, then it is qualified."

401(k)

The most famous of these programs in today's world is the 401(k). The basics of the program are pretty simple. The IRS allows you, in cooperation with your employer, to put a certain percentage of your income into a specified group of investments before the money is taxed and before the money makes it into your checking account. In addition, they also allow your employer to put money into the accounts, on your behalf, tax-free.

Well, for the moment, at least.

As always, the government gets its money at some point. In this case, you are taxed when you withdraw the money. It all comes out as income tax. This creates two issues. First, the I.R.S. limits your access to the money; otherwise, it charges you a penalty. And, second, for many people in the highest tax brackets, it becomes a bit of a trap.

Think of it this way: when you are young, you have tax deductions, such as children, mortgage interest and maybe contributions to an I.R.A. However, when you retire, you may have very little in the way of deductions, your tax bracket may be unchanged and you will be taxed on withdrawals you make from certain retirement accounts like the 401(k) or traditional

I.R.A. Unless you dramatically cut your pre-retirement lifestyle, your tax bill may even go up in certain years if you incur large expenses.

This is the point when most people ask whether they should even contribute to a 410(k). You definitely should if you are receiving a match. You should always invest at least up to that point. After that, it gets a little more complicated and you need to consider your income level and how much you are saving elsewhere.

So before we max out the 401(k), let's look at what other options are available.

Roth I.R.A.

For most people, the best retirement option after the match is the Roth I.R.A. (assuming your AGI is under the threshold; this changes almost every year so check with your tax adviser). The Roth I.R.A. is the anti-traditional 401(k). With the 401(k), you get all of the tax breaks initially; your income is tax-deferred going into the account and turns into taxable income coming out. With the Roth, you pay income taxes on the money you deposit into the account as you normally would. But when you pull the money out, after age 59 ½, it is tax-free!!

"For most people, the best retirement option after the match is the Roth I.R.A."

Let's assume you put the money into the account in 2009 and the law that year allowed a maximum investment of $5,000 with a catch-up provision of an additional $1,000 if you are over 50. For my clients who are having an off year, this is a dream come true. Why? Because when you go to take the money out, as long as you are past 59½, no taxes are due! This is one of the reasons that the I.R.S. limits the amount we can put in.

Where do I tell my clients to put their money?

First, invest in the 401(k) to the match; nothing beats free money from your employer. Next, if you are eligible, max out your Roth I.R.A. Once you have maxed out your Roth I.R.A., go back to the 401(k) and put as much into it as you can afford. You should shoot for a minimum of 10 percent of your salary, deferred every year in I.R.A.s or 401(k)s.

"First, invest in the 401(k) to the match; nothing beats free money from

your employer. Next, if you are eligible, max out your Roth I.R.A. Once you have maxed out your Roth I.R.A., go back to the 401(k) and put as much into it as you can afford."

Traditional I.R.A.

The traditional I.R.A. works similarly to the 401(k) except that there is no match and the money generally hits your checking account where you then invest it and get your write-off at the end of the year. Since there is no match, go with the 401(k) first. At that point, it becomes a question as to whether you want to contribute to a traditional I.R.A. or a Roth I.R.A. The guidelines for the traditional I.R.A. are more restrictive and unless you feel certain you are going to be in a lower tax bracket in retirement, stick with the Roth, even if you are eligible to participate in the traditional I.R.A.

The reason that most of my clients end up with the traditional I.R.A. is that when you separate from your employer, you can roll over the old 401(k) into a traditional I.R.A., which allows greater control and more investment choices.

457, 403(b), Simple I.R.A., SEP, etc.

Almost all other retirement programs are a variation on the 401(k) theme. Although the differences can be important, they don't impact enough people to address them here. So if your employer offers something different just check to make sure they are ERISA-compliant. If they are, the golden rule is that you are probably better off participating than not participating.

Non-qualified accounts

Non-qualified accounts, for simplicity's sake, generally offer little or no tax advantage, but they do offer more flexibility.

The Savings Account

"Savings accounts" earn interest, have little risk, and allow you easy access to your money. Money market accounts also fall into this category. Unfortunately you get taxed on the income every year. These are not retirement accounts (or at least they should not be). They are cash reserves, car savings, or savings for any large purchase that you may need to make in the next five years; otherwise, you should invest for the longer term. Whenever you are putting money aside for a rainy day or for a large purchase, and are more concerned about accessibility than growth, a savings account is the way to go.

Investment Accounts

After you leave the low-risk, low-return saving accounts, the field of investments, tax treatments and the levels of risk open up.

Bonds

Bonds can potentially produce income from both dividends and capital gains, but they also have risk. Short-term U.S. treasuries offer the least risk, but they also have the lowest returns. Bonds issued by municipalities also offer lower returns, but they normally have the advantage of no federal income tax. Corporate bonds offer the highest returns, but they also have the highest risk of default.

Municipal bonds are second-tier bonds. Most states, counties, cities, and government projects have little risk since they normally can go to their tax base and raise taxes to generate more income to pay the bonds if necessary. But there are definitely different levels of risks with municipal bonds.

Generally considered the safest are general obligation bonds (GO Bonds). A GO bond is backed by the government agency that issues it and even if the associated project falls flat, the municipality still has the general obligation to pay it to term out of its general revenues.

Next would be revenue bonds. A revenue bond is generally tied to one specific function (e.g., a sewer system, hospital, or even a sports complex). If the revenues for that function can't cover the bond, there is the potential for that bond to default. A default of any type of municipal bond is rare but it does happen. Whether you are looking at GO bonds or revenue bonds, the credit score of the bond is a helpful way to determine its risk. The higher the rating, the better (in most situations).

Corporate bonds offer the most risk and generally offer the highest potential for return. By definition, they offer more risk because businesses go out of business everyday while the United States and its municipalities do not. Additionally we have to choose to purchase the goods that corporations sell us and, over time, even companies that seemed great can fail. Fifty years ago, no one could imagine that the Big Three U.S. automakers might fail, and now we wonder how much government assistance it will take to keep them afloat. Governments have a little more control; they can generate revenue by taxing us whether we like it or not. This makes them a better long-term bet.

Equities, better known as stocks, are another option. They offer much greater short-term risk, but they have the potential for greater long-term rewards such as dividend yields and tax advantages.

How Do You Invest?

For convenience and diversification needs, most people start out investing in open-ended mutual funds. Most mutual fund companies will allow you to start with as little as $100 on a monthly draft or with a single lump sum of $2,000. There are a number of well-known companies, like Morningstar, that can assist you with making good choices. But remember that even if a fund has done well in the past, it may not be appropriate for you - or continue its success into the future. Ranking is just one of the tools professional advisors use to rate a fund.

"For convenience and diversification needs, most people start out investing in open-ended mutual funds."

Mutual funds* can be purchased in a variety of ways. The choice is dependent upon how active you want to be in the decision-making process, how much risk you want to take, how much time you want to spend doing it, and whether you are set on going it alone or would prefer professional advice.

*Mutual Fund values fluctuate so that an investor's shares, when redeemed, may be worth more or less than their original cost.

Chapter 3

How to Hire a Financial Advisor

First of all, the do-it-yourself (DIY) approach, especially in the early years, is not necessarily a bad decision. You may have little to invest and that may make it more difficult for you to get a top-rated advisor. Second, for most of my clients, especially in the early years, you really are only looking for core investments. If you only have $2,000 to invest, diversification is somewhat of a moot point; you need to start building a solid core. This can be done either through quality, managed funds or a product that strictly follows an index.

Index Investing

For most DIYers, I recommend purchasing one of the readily available index funds or ETFs, specifically following the S&P 500 index. For most Americans, this will be the core of their investments for years.

Can you find investments that consistently beat this index (although there is no guarantee)?

Certainly, but this is one of those situations when an individual is more likely to make the mistake of chasing returns than a pro would be. Chasing returns is the tendency to choose last year's winner rather than looking forward to next year's winner.

"For most DIYers, I recommend purchasing one of the readily available index funds or ETFs, specifically following the S&P 500 index. For most Americans, this will be the core of their investments for years."

Most advisors will tell you that the market runs in cycles. One of the worst things you can do is buy at the end of each cycle. You and your advisor do not have to be in the front position of every market trend to perform well, but you do not want to be the last person to buy into a cycle because when the cycle ends, it can hurt.

So unless you are working with an advisor, I recommend an investment that tracks a core index. As I said before, you can find something that will outperform the index, but it may still be a poor investment from a time-management standpoint. Remember, a professional advisor is not just tracking the market trends for you, but for their entire client base. It is cost-effective for them to look beyond the basics while, for you, it isn't.

Several, if not most, of my clients were, at one time, DIYers. There are definitely appropriate times for you to go it alone and ultimately you have to live with your results and not your advisor. What that means is that even if you are handing over every one of your financial decisions to someone else, you still made the most important decision: to trust that specific individual with your finances. Therefore, to a certain degree, no one ever stops being a DIYer.

Nevertheless, everyone should understand that there is a difference between things you *can* do and things you *should* do for yourself. One day, when discussing this with a client named Bill, he responded that it is the same in his profession. "Any doctor would treat a family member if they got a cut on the finger. It would not be an issue to apply a Band-Aid. But none of them would, or at least should, do open-heart surgery on themselves or a loved one."

Bill then got a wicked smile and joked that he might consider open-heart surgery on a loved one if the patient was, for example, his mother-in-law. Bill's smile was short-lived. His wife quickly quipped back that she wasn't sure her mother counted as one of his "loved ones."

Bill may have ended up on the couch that night.

Most financial advisors know that most everyone has blind spots when it comes to financial planning. It could be with insurance (some folks believe they are going to live forever) or equities. The other thing few DIYers take into consideration is the time commitment required to learn the skills necessary to compete with professional advisors.

"Most financial advisors know that most everyone has blind spots when it comes to financial planning."

Most true DIYers become good at one part of the financial puzzle, but leave themselves open to either unnecessary risk or lower returns. Alternative products may be necessary to balance portfolios or lower risk, but few individual investors follow, or can even access, them without a pro's help. However, if you are still determined, start with something small; this way, if you make a mistake, you can recover.

"Most true DIYers become good at one part of the financial puzzle, but leave themselves open to either unnecessary risk or lower returns."

The Non-Professional Advisor (Better known as your friend, parent, or wise Uncle Wilbur)

"The advice of friends must be received with a judicious reserve; we must not give ourselves up to it and follow it blindly, whether right or wrong."
    ~Pierre Charron

"Many receive advice, few profit by it."
    ~Publilius Syrus (~100 BC), Maxims

"Never take the advice of someone who has not had your kind of trouble."
    ~Sidney J. Harris

It never fails to give me a chuckle when a client tells me that a co-worker has given him a hot tip. It seems that there is a person in everyone's life that gives the impression (whether on purpose or not) that they are a financial genius.

Football and Cheesecake

Unfortunately even if a friend has done well for himself or herself, it has little bearing on whether or not his or her advice will do well for you. Just as in sports, being a good player does not make you a good coach, or for that matter, even a good player at the next level. In high school, I was judged a good athlete and made all-conference in football. Does that mean I should have gone pro? At 5'9" and 160 pounds, only if I was insane. Today the average kicker on a high school team is probably 50 pounds heavier than I was in high school.

However, if a person seems to do well financially then everyone assumes they are competent to dispense financial advice. This simply is not the case, just like my successes in high school did not entitle me to become a professional coach. It is the *knowledge* and *training* about the entire game, not just a personal experience, that makes a coach successful.

Similarly if a friend is truly proficient in one area of investing, you are still at risk when following his or her advice.

A true financial planner weighs the pros and cons of all financial products, and understands how to apply them to a client's unique situation. This is far different from the friend who may have generated significant wealth in real estate, for example, and suggests a similar strategy for you even if the market has changed or you do not have the time or resources to put into it.

"A true financial planner weighs the pros and cons of all financial products, and understands how to apply them to a client's unique situation."

We have all had this experience. At one time or another, we have all been told about a great restaurant. You know the one you simply "must try," only to find out it is crawling with kids. The food may be great, but if your goal is a romantic evening, the ambiance leaves a lot to be desired.

The problem is not the restaurant but the circumstances. The family that recommended the restaurant may have found it ideal because they were comfortable and couldn't hear their kids screaming over everyone else's. It would have been a great recommendation for another family. But if your goal was to have a romantic evening, I think not.

Those of us with families have also had the reverse happen. After a soccer match, we head with the kids in tow into what we were told was a great casual restaurant, only to find out the wine list is two pages long and that they don't have a children's menu. Again both of these restaurants may be fabulous, and the referrer may have excellent taste. But neither of those facts makes the recommendation suitable for your situation at that specific time.

In reality, almost every financial product was perfectly designed for someone. The question is whether you are that someone. And if you are, is this the right time? For this reason, no matter how good the friend, this person is likely to see your situation as being the same and that can lead to both the loss of money and the loss of a friend.

"In reality, almost every financial product was perfectly designed for someone. The question is whether you are that someone."

Even if you have someone who can see past their personal situation, there remains one more catch: everyone naturally discounts what they have been unsuccessful at, or what they do not understand. This means the more complicated the concept, the more likely someone else is going to say you should never do it. This is especially true for us guys. The cliché about a man never asking for directions all too often holds true for financial matters as well. Very few men like to admit to what they don't know.

Unfortunately, that confusion can extend to professional advisors. When you talk with someone who has had a financial setback due to incompetency, he or she generally says that the advisor blamed the product. Yet the fault all too often belongs with the advisor. Take, for example, permanent insurance. For many people in the right tax bracket, it can be a phenomenal solution. But there are many incompetent people selling it. So it has earned a bad reputation.

Complexity, mixed with highly competitive commissions, has created more than one problem over the years. However if you review the estate plans of the wealthiest Americans, you'd almost always find permanent insurance in one of its various forms. The key is in working with competent agents and not rookies or fly-by-night companies. It normally isn't the product that's the problem; the problem is how the product is used.

"It normally isn't the product that's the problem; the problem is how the product is used."

So just remember that the more complex a product is, the greater the likelihood that someone will say something bad about it. And whether it's a personal preference or a lack of knowledge, once a person's mind is made up, there is little anyone can do to change it. My wife, Dianne, is that way about cheesecake. Being a New Yorker and having a great aunt who literally chased her other great aunt around the Thanksgiving table one year because she dared to cut one of her homemade cheesecakes with a knife instead of a string, it is safe to say that she and her entire family are a little picky about their cheesecakes.

So to my wife, there is only one type of cheesecake. Also, a true New York cheesecake can't be desecrated with a topping. And it wouldn't dare use the name "cheesecake" if it isn't at least three inches tall (anything less would be a cheese pie, I guess). And, of course, there is the texture, which I dare not try to describe and risk getting it wrong.

When Dianne finds a restaurant that offers that true New York cheesecake, it becomes an almost religious experience for her and a miserable one for me. Unfortunately, I hate cheesecake, and she knows this. Yet she can't help but try to force it down my throat when she finds one that meets her strict guidelines. Think of this the next time you hear someone talking about all of the money that he or she made with a particular stock or mutual fund. While it may have worked for them, it may not work for you. And just because a person likes a specific product, doesn't mean it will be right for you.

Super Genius

Back when I had just started my practice, there was a client - we'll call him Richard – who, every time he came in to see me, kept bragging to me about how well he was doing at picking stocks. He would do this every time he came in to see me - it never ceased to amaze me. The stories Richard would tell me of how he picked some little stock that tripled in a week made me feel both insecure and a little green with envy. After a while, I was beginning to doubt my own abilities and wondered why this equities genius was working with a schmuck like me. It was about that time that Richard's C.P.A. called me and asked if there were any gains that could be harvested (for tax reasons) before year-end from the accounts that I managed for Richard.

Even though the question confused me (because you normally harvest losses), I responded that Richard's account was up and we had some relatively large gains that we could take. Frankly, the account had done great in an average market. But I was sure that Richard's personal account had done much better.

Being a rookie and again feeling very much like a schmuck, I asked the obvious question. "Why do you need me to harvest gains with all the great picks Richard has made over the last year?" His C.P.A. started laughing so hard that I thought he was going to hyperventilate. It must have taken him 15 minutes to regain his composure. But when he eventually caught his breath, he confided in me that Richard had lost over $50,000 in the market that year.

The C.P.A. was hoping the accounts managed by me would allow us to harvest enough gains to take advantage of the tax losses that Richard had generated. Astonished, I questioned him about the stories Richard had told me. Again the C.P.A. laughed. He went on to explain that Richard did pick winners on a relatively frequent basis. In fact, since he traded daily, he averaged around one per week. The problem was that over the past 20 years, the C.P.A. could not remember Richard having a single positive year. The C.P.A. said that Richard always picked more losers than winners; however, Richard never bragged about the losers.

Having several opportunities to socialize with Richard and several of his associates, it did not take me long to realize that many of his associates unquestioningly followed Richard's investment advice, even though they commonly stated that they could never match his returns. They actually felt lucky when they just broke even. And during the whole time we worked together, Richard never let on that he wasn't doing any better than they were.

Unfortunately, this story happens all too frequently. People often discuss their winners, but seldom mention their losers. This inequity leaves their friends and colleagues with a false sense of their accomplishments and an unjustified willingness to follow their lead. The truth of the matter is that unless a person is in your exact position and you want the exact results they are getting, their advice is useless. Worse yet, it may even be dangerous.

Betamax

Let's go back a couple of years - okay, *decades* - for one more analogy. We have two brothers, Bert and Ernie. Bert buys a Betamax and Ernie buys a VCR. At the time of purchase, both Bert *and* Ernie would tell you that they have the best, most cutting-edge product ever. And at the time of purchase, they do.

However, a few years later, after Betamax has collapsed, Bert (the Betamax guy) tells you to avoid buying new technology because it never works out. On the other hand, Ernie, the VCR guy, swears that the VCR is the best purchase he's ever made. Ask Bert and Ernie about DVDs and they roll their eyes. Ask Bert's grandson and he laughs and says, "DVDs? They are so 90s! Have you looked at Blu-Ray?"

Investments can change just as fast.

Getting the Right Advice

Up until this point, you probably have had the impression that you should never talk to anyone about your finances or give any recommendations yourself. That assumption, however, is far from the truth. I believe you should get recommendations from friends, family members and coworkers in two specific ways. First, see if they love their advisors. If they do, then ask about those relationships and what they like the most - and least - about how their advisors work. If they are extremely happy, ask if they will give referrals. Do the same in return.

Why most people ask each other for product advice, instead of asking for a referral to a competent advisor, is beyond me. It would be a little like asking someone who was cured from a specific disease about the drugs he or she took instead of the doctor who remedied the problem. Shouldn't you let the doctor diagnose your specific condition and prescribe what will work best for you? Can you just imagine receiving a prescription based upon the diagnosis of the referring patient?

Chapter 4

How to Avoid the Paper Chase

Had you graduated from school 10 years ago, we'd still have been talking about identify theft. However, the focus at the time was primarily on vulnerabilities in our "pay-by-paper" society. Today, those associated risks have only been compounded by the modern-day worries and, additionally, staying on top of both paper *and* electronic documents can get tough.

But this all remains a critical piece of financial management. So let's roll up our sleeves and get started.

First of all, please buy a paper shredder and get into the habit of shredding all of your old financial documents, bills, receipts, bank statements and credit card offers when you no longer need them. These days, I pretty much shred any piece of mail with my name on it when I no longer need it. Also, don't casually carry around any documents bearing your social security number. Lock them up in a safe or safety deposit box.

"First of all, please buy a paper shredder and get into the habit of

shredding all of your old financial documents, bills, receipts, bank statements and credit card offers when you no longer need them."

Should you become a victim of identity theft, Ryan recommends reporting it at www.ic3.gov. This enables the FBI to build cases. Also, anomalies on your credit report tend to be the first sign that you're a victim, so you really should check your report annually. Ryan recommends going to www.annualcreditreport.com and getting one free report every year.

"Should you become a victim of identity theft, Ryan recommends reporting it at www.ic3.gov."

No matter how careful you are, you will probably sooner or later be impacted by a data breach via a national retailer, bank, your alma mater, etc. Don't panic, but do be proactive. Do all of the recommended steps contained in the notification letter and contact the credit bureaus. They have programs that can help.

Equifax, one of the three credit bureaus, explained some of the options to me. You can request a *security freeze* to prevent your credit report from being shared with many, if not most, third parties. The cost varies by state, but probably won't exceed $10 and it's generally a free service if you've been a victim of identity theft. The security freeze can only be requested by you, will remain on your file until you request otherwise and can only be removed or suspended by you again, there may be small fees for making changes).

You have several options if you need to request a security freeze. You can go online at https://www.freeze.equifax.com; request it by phone, at 1-800-685- 1111 (New York residents, 1-800-349-9960); or request it by mail at:

Equifax Security Freeze
P.O. Box 105788
Atlanta, Georgia 30348

For additional security freezes, you will need to contact the other credit bureaus directly:

TransUnion

Fraud Victim Assistance

P.O. Box 6790

Fullerton, CA 92834

Experian

Experian Security Freeze

P.O. Box 9554

Allen, TX 75013

You can add a *fraud alert* to your file to give a heads-up to creditors that you've been victimized, which enables them to take preventive steps and work harder to confirm your identity before opening new accounts in your name, issuing new cards and increasing new credit limits. You can arrange to have a 90-day fraud alert, or request an extended one that lasts seven years.

"You can add a *fraud alert* to your file to give a heads-up to creditors that you've been victimized, which enables them to take preventive steps and work harder to confirm your identity before opening new

accounts in your name, issuing new cards and increasing new credit limits."

The good news, here, is that when you add a fraud alert to your file with Equifax, they will generally contact the other two credit bureaus within 24 hours to have it added to your files with TransUnion and Experian. To place an initial, 90-day fraud alert or an active-duty alert (for military personnel) online with Equifax, please go to: https://www.alerts.equifax.com. You can also call 1- 888-766-0008 or send a letter to:

Equifax Consumer Fraud Division
P.O. Box 740256
Atlanta, GA 30374

You will need to have two forms of ID when making your request. Fortunately, the two lists include a wide range of options, including a driver's license, pay stub, utility bill, passport, birth certificate, mortgage statement and a bank statement. You can find more information at www.equifax.com.

Managing Paperwork

This leaves us with documents you need to keep. For all of us, this means current and past tax returns, all supporting documents and, for small businesses, all of the receipts, bills and financial statements associated with your return. Combine all of this with your monthly bills, car title, house deed, legal documents, medical documents, travel research and other reference documents and you will quickly understand the need for a good filing system.

Some important documents that I suggest you store in a safety deposit box at your bank include your:

> Passport
> Social Security card
> House deed
> Birth certificate
> Car title
> Will
> Power of attorney document

This will not only help keep you organized, but will also train your mind to look for, and store, all key documents in one safe and secure place. Likewise, I also recommend that you store all external hard drives, containing your electronic documents, in a safe within your home. For other documents, I recommend getting a standard four-drawer filing cabinet, hanging folders, labels and begin organizing the paperwork. Here are some key files to get you started:

- Bank statements
- Bill statements
- Investment statements
- Contracts
- Tax information
- Medical documents
- Health insurance documents
- School records

If you need to save your receipts for expense reports or tax write-offs, just get two basic accordion files at an office-supply store and divvy up your receipts by month, pocket by pocket, using one accordion file for personal receipts and one for business. If you love color, you can jazz it up with sources like Office Candy, http://www.officecandy.com. The key thing is to just do it.

"The key thing is to just do it."

For the receipts you gather while on the go, I recommend you get a wallet or a small clutch. When the satchel gets stuffed, simply empty it into the appropriate pockets within your accordion files. Also, if you need to track your miles (for your Schedule C or expense report) and have an iPad with you most of the time, try the Numbers app for noting dates, distances and purposes of your travel. (The rule of thumb is to keep your electronic devices in one bag and keep that bag on you at all times, outside of the house.)

When it comes to managing your mail, toss your junk mail into a recycling container as soon as it arrives. Otherwise, it ends up burying important letters, bills and statements. And since it piles up so quickly, it will also make you feel perpetually behind, which is exactly what we are trying to avoid.

"When it comes to managing your mail, toss your junk mail into a recycling container as soon as it arrives."

Your best bet is to limit what shows up in the first place. Start again with the credit bureaus since they may otherwise share details in your files with certain businesses, like credit card companies. If you opt out with Equifax, they will again share your request with the other two reporting agencies. You can call 1-888- 5-OPT OUT or write Equifax (with your name, address, social security number and signature) at:

Equifax Information Services
P.O. Box 740123
Atlanta, GA 30374-0123

For paperwork requiring a response - like bills, invitations, phone messages, coupons, shopping lists, catalogues and birth announcements - keep a small file box on your desk with 10 or so labeled, hanging folders. This will enable you to manage the paperwork in an orderly fashion. Again, OfficeCandy.com and ContainerStore.com have attractive options if that's important to you.

The key, according to professional organizers, is that you store your incoming paperwork in a way that feels right to you because if you don't like your system, you won't use it. This also goes for all of the online statements and bills. They require their own filing system.

Consider automated drafts for your monthly bills (using your credit card) as it will save you time. My bank, SunTrust, not only has bill pay, but also an app that covers most of my banking needs. The app enables me to deposit a check remotely (by just taking a picture of it), check balances, pay bills, transfer money, and find the nearest ATM.

But even with a good electronic system for managing your income and outgo, review your statements every month and, of course, respond quickly when you catch any errors. I also like using account-aggregation software - with a vault to store information electronically, such as copies of wills, passports, insurance contracts, and power of attorney documents. And don't forget to archive your electronic statements - either together or in separate files (e.g., water, gas, bank, insurance, investment and cell phone). All of this will enable you to manage your email better. Otherwise, inbox messages quickly pile up, like paperwork, leaving you feeling perpetually behind, buried and not on top of things.

"Disorganization is a pernicious lifestyle that will sacrifice the quality of your life ..."

You will find many professionals lack good filing systems. They are the ones who are constantly wasting time, inefficient and frustrated. And it doesn't end with the paperwork. The perpetually disorganized will often have messy offices, cars, debt, overdue tax bills - even messy appearances. Incessant disorganization is a pernicious lifestyle that will sacrifice the quality of your life, and impact your ability to effectively plan for your future, see the big picture and enact realistic and effective plans for your money over the short- and long-term. So managing your paperwork is the foundation of good financial management.

Now, onward and upward ...

Chapter 5

How to Avoid the Credit Card Trap

"Adulthood - The point where your parents won't let you move back home even though all you own is a bean bag"

~Me

As you become established professionally and personally, you are probably going to develop an affinity for consumer goods. For this reason, this is also the point when many consumers first encounter non-student loan debt. But as with everything in life, the key is to find a balance. So, here are some of the rules that can save you from a headache and potentially even a divorce. (After all, money issues are the leading cause of divorce and this is especially true for young professionals. The more dramatic a change in income, the greater the stress can be - especially if you and your spouse are not working together to achieve common financial goals.)

First of all, I am about to do something I personally abhor: make a blanket statement. But here is my one and only blanket statement:

Credit cards are dangerous!!!

It may sound simplistic, but these little pieces of plastic were created by the devil himself! Okay, I may be exaggerating a little bit, but not much.

Here is why:

1. You spend more!!!!

Picture yourself walking into a convenience store right after eating lunch at your favorite restaurant. You head straight for the gum and search the aisle for your favorite brand, only to realize that you are 15 cents short. Since you've decided that you really need the gum, out comes the plastic. After all, who wants to walk all the way to the car for a measly 15 cents? Not you. You have that appointment in 15 minutes and you need your gum now!

However, there is no way you are just going to charge a buck. So you decide to get a drink as well. You're thirsty right?

You are probably smart enough to know where this is going.

For most people, the charging threshold is right around $5. So you collect enough stuff to reach that $5 mark and make your way to the counter.

Research shows that when a person uses a credit card instead of cash, their spending goes up between 10 and 30 percent on average. This is true whether you are at the convenience store or buying furniture. Of course, the furniture store loves it when you sign up for their cards. Do you really think they are giving you a bargain if they offer you 10 percent off of your first purchase and no payments until the new millennium? They do it because they know you are not only going to buy the couch (which you may have had enough cash to pay for immediately), but you are also going to buy a couple of extras, like those throw pillows that match perfectly.

"Research shows that when a person uses a credit card instead of cash, their spending goes up between 10 and 30 percent on average."

So the amount of money you were *planning* on spending has now doubled. The furniture store is also banking on the fact that you are going to be the typical consumer and not quite have everything paid off by the end of the free interest period -

chances are they are going to be right. The average consumer seldom gets everything paid off by the end of the term.

Even if you are disciplined enough to pay everything off on time, they still have marked your purchases up enough to cover the financing anyway. However, you can make some smart moves of your own. If you follow two simple rules, you can avoid most of the mistakes that the average person makes.

The Consumer Debt Rules:

> ➢ Whatever you buy should be paid off before you finish using it.
> ➢ Always refer to Rule #1.

Let's look at some quick examples. If you go out to dinner, pay with cash. A trip to the movies? Pay with cash. Going to a football game? Pay with cash once again. The same holds true for groceries, gas, clothes, or anything that will no longer be of use once the bill arrives.

Understandably, some big-ticket items, like cars (especially early in your career), may cause you to take on some debt. However, you still need to plan to have the car paid off before getting your *next* car. If you cannot do so, then you are looking at a car that is too expensive for your budget.

The four RULES for your credit card:

1. Every time you make a purchase, immediately transfer money from your checking account to your credit card.
2. Use your credit card for ongoing bills that you know you are going to have every month.
3. Pay your credit card off every month.
4. Use your credit card for reimbursable business expenses.

Why Rule #1: This way you can use your credit card like you would an ATM card. With online bill pay, it is easy. You also avoid unpleasant surprises in the mail by using this technique. But best of all, it will force you to look at your checking account when you make the transfer, making you more aware of what your current balance is.

Why Rule #2: Use it for ongoing bills like your cell phone. You can then set up your bill pay to send a check to the credit card company to pay off that portion of your bill automatically.

Why Rule #3: No matter what, *always* pay your credit card bill off every month, even if you have to dip into savings to do so. Once you start carrying a balance, it becomes easier and easier to rationalize larger and larger balances, so make a sacrifice and dip into savings. This is true even if the credit card company is offering you zero percent interest. Their hope is that you will be so used to carrying the balance that when the rate goes up, you will suffer from any of the following:

> Not having the cash to pay it off.

> Having the cash, but not noticing the rate change.

> Being so used to carrying the balance, it would actually feel odd not to have one.

More than once, new clients have walked into my office with over $100,000 in their checking accounts - earning 1 percent - and credit card bills north of $50,000, costing them 15 percent. I don't know about you, but I'm pretty sure the bank likes those customers.

"No matter what, *always* pay your credit card bill off every month, even if you have to dip into savings to do so."

Why Rule #4: Your company should reimburse you before the bill is due. Then just transfer the entire amount of the reimbursement check to the credit card company. Try to use a separate card for this purpose. That way, you can then make certain you are in balance every month and you don't have to worry about picking personal expenses out of the business ones. You get the points; they get the bill.

2. The points don't matter!!

In my opinion, credit card points, miles and credits may be the biggest marketing rip-off of the last 15 years. Let's use a little logic here. I think we can all agree on one fact and that is that the credit card companies are not in the business of giving money away. In other words, the points programs make them more profitable, not less. If they are more profitable, that means you are less profitable. Even if you make the argument that you pay your bill off every month, the likelihood is that you still spend somewhere between 10 and 30 percent more with a credit card than with cash. Think if you had invested 10 percent of your monthly bill into an average mutual fund earning 8 percent per year. How much would you have ended up with? That additional savings would have provided a lot more trips to the Bahamas than your points program ever would have!

If you have already succumbed to the credit bug, it's time for immediate action! Remove your credit cards from your wallet or purse and leave them at home. It sounds easy, doesn't it? But most people who have the credit bug don't last a month. If you have tried and failed in a moment of weakness, I recommend the extremely corny technique of freezing them. It amazes me that those words ever came out of my mouth, and the first time I suggested it, I wasn't even serious. However, when I realized that my clients, Judy and John, felt that they had no willpower - but were uncomfortable with not having any credit available for emergencies - it actually started to make sense to me. This simple action became their cooling-off period before a purchase. It worked perfectly.

If you are already carrying credit card debt, this is the first debt you need to pay off. If possible, move the balances to the cards with the lowest rates and then aggressively pay the debt down. Make *no* big purchases while you have credit card debt and that includes planning vacations.

"Make *no* big purchases while you have credit card debt and that includes planning vacations."

Book Review

Financial Peace by Dave Ramsey. Dave's target market is people who have had significant problems with debt. I love his no-nonsense approach to dealing with debt and getting out of the hole. All of his books are simple, straightforward, and easy to read. If you are having a hard time controlling debt, any of Dave's books can really help.

Chapter 6

How to Buy and Furnish Your First Home

The American dream has always been homeownership. Why should it be any different today?

For most people, a home is their largest, most important and most expensive purchase. However, today we are taking on bigger responsibilities faster and faster. Instead of growing into our parents' lifestyles over decades, we want it all now. Additionally, "keeping up with the Joneses" has become a major cultural issue. Author and radio personality Dave Ramsey is famous for saying that his listeners and readers "should **live like no one else,** *so you can live like no one else.*" He believes, as do I, that consumerism and debt are problems. I personally believe that if you are willing to give up a little of your consumerism today, you will be able to achieve your goals earlier and still live a comfortable lifestyle. Delayed gratification actually allows for greater gratification over your life.

What I am politely trying to say is: ***Do not over buy!***

Everyone will tell you what a great investment your home is, but if you have to take out your credit cards to buy groceries then you are in over your head. So here are a few rules of thumb so your dream home doesn't become your personal money pit.

The Five Laws of Purchasing Your First Home

1. Have a down payment
2. Live the life *before* you go shopping
3. Don't get a "stupid" mortgage (I will go into depth below)
4. Only furnish what you can afford
5. Save green by going green

Law #1: The Down Payment? You better have one!

Let's face it, if you wait to have 20 percent for your down payment, you might be retired before you ever move in. Having said that, you should have, at a minimum, 5 percent. With an additional 10 percent (or more) in the bank for moving expenses.

On the flip side you should never have more than 20 percent equity in your home. Because I am trying to keep this book short and don't want to write an additional 100 pages on the subject, a great book to read, which takes a deep dive into this subject, is *Missed Fortune 101* by Douglas Andrew.

"On the flip side you should never have more than 20 percent equity in your home."

Book Review

Missed Fortune 101 by Douglas Andrew. Doug's book is generally on the money and illustrates one of the best methods for maximizing the value of underutilized assets. The only two places our views differ are on his overuse of insurance and his treatment of qualified plans. Overall a great read and a real eye-opener for most people! Just remember one size does not fit all!

Although there are good financial reasons not to have more than 20 percent equity in your home, there is something to be said for peace of mind. So if you think the grass will be greener in the yard of a paid-off house, by all means I think you should go for it. Just be certain to understand what you are giving up in return.

For the purposes of this book, moving expenses include everything you need to buy when you move in: furniture, appliances, yard supplies, "the works". The bad news is that 10 percent will probably not cover all of your start-up costs to move and completely furnish a new home. This means you have to give up something; the last thing you want is to take on extra debt for that pretty leather couch.

So, when you have spent your 10 percent cushion, do not go into debt for a couch or any other miscellaneous item! Even if the furniture store you love is offering no payments and no interest for five years, it is not worth the future pain; just don't do it. Instead, save and pay cash when you have the money.

If you find that you cannot fully furnish your home with the cash you have set aside, then it is time to set some priorities. The easiest way to prioritize your next purchase is to determine the rooms you can't live without. For example, if part of your dream is entertaining every weekend, then you should complete the rooms you will be entertaining in first and skip the bedrooms.

"If you find that you cannot fully furnish your home with the cash you

have set aside then it is time to set some priorities."

If you are not the master entertainer, then work on the rooms you and your family plan on using the most. Maybe it is the playroom or a bedroom. Perhaps a big screen TV means that a media room takes priority over a formal dining room. Do whatever works for you.

Law #2: Live the life *before* you go shopping

"How much home can I afford?"

The problem when you ask this question is that you always get a different answer. The banks will say you are approved for one thing while Uncle Bob says another. The fact is that none of these numbers really matter. Take my family as an example. I am writing a book, tuition is coming due for private schools, my wife and I enjoy traveling, and a night out will easily cost us well over $100.

So if I accepted the maximum loan the bank allowed, I would be stuck at home eating Ramen noodles and, frankly, I like living an enjoyable lifestyle more than I like my house. However, several of my friends are not big travelers, only go out occasionally, and are your basic homebodies. Being house poor isn't part of their vocabularies. They love their homes and if it takes Ramen noodles for them to live there, they are more than happy to oblige.

This leads us back to the question of how much you should spend, and my response is very pragmatic: Live the life.

It sounds simple, but before you decide whether to buy a $1,000,000 or $250,000 home, you should live the life. With the $1,000,000 home, you may need to cook Ramen noodles every day for the next 30 years because you can barely make the mortgage payment. On the flip side, with the $250,000 home, you may be able to travel the world. But there is nowhere near enough room to have all of your family and friends over for dinner. So, you must LIVE THE LIFE!

The reality, and one of the underlying themes of this book, is that each person is different - so you should ignore all of them and focus on living *your* life. The best method is to use what I call the "Live the Life" method. It really is both simple and powerful.

"The best method is to use what I call the 'Live the Life' method. It really is both simple and powerful."

First, you decide what type of house you want and possibly even the exact neighborhood you want to live in. At this point, any decent Realtor can determine the approximate costs for that home and neighborhood. Be certain to include the mortgage, taxes, utilities, insurance, and any other costs, such as lawn care (if you are not a DIYer).

You then subtract the current living expenses for your current residence and start saving the difference on a monthly basis. You need to do this for a minimum of six months. Don't buy until you have completed the six-month period.

You may find that the new house is too expensive. Or you may find that you have found the perfect lifestyle and the new budget fits your family perfectly. Either way, it will take you about six months to know for sure.

Obviously, if you can't save the difference between your current expenses and your projected expenses, then you are overshooting. Don't kid yourself. If you are not comfortable living on the budget before you move in, what makes you think you will be able to do it *after* you move in? What would you give up when you move that you are unwilling to give up now?

You will be better off either picking a different home or waiting until you can afford the home of your dreams. Also, there is nothing wrong with renting. It allows you to save money for a later purchase, buys you time to work on, or establish, your credit rating and generally covers all of the maintenance issues.

Law #3: Don't get a "stupid" mortgage!

Okay, you have picked the neighborhood and are "Living the Life." You have double-checked your figures to make certain that you are not underestimating your expenses. Now you need to understand your mortgage choices.

This has become more complicated than passing the bar exam!

So here's a quick primer on the most common types of mortgages and my recommendations.

30-year

The 30-year fixed mortgage is both your banker's and your parents' favorite.

Why?

Well, for the banker, they normally get to charge you a higher rate with a 30-year loan than with any other mortgage. Because you can potentially take the full 30 years to pay, the bank needs a higher rate to justify the liability. No one can predict where the rates will be 20 years from now, so they have to hedge today by charging more to cover that risk (compared to a mortgage with a rate that resets regularly).

However, they know statistically that you are probably going to move or refinance in less than seven years. Today's average is closer to five years than it is seven years. In other words, they get to charge you a higher rate today because you *could* pay for 30 years. However, they know the odds are very slim that you will stay in your home long enough to take advantage of it.

This fact makes a 30-year fixed mortgage a pretty good deal for the bank.

If it is that profitable for the bank, why does everyone love it so much? Why did your parents have one and why are they adamant that you get one? The reason is that it was probably their first mortgage and it was probably your grandparents' *only* mortgage.

Of course your grandparents probably had no choice; when they got their first mortgage, there were very few options. Additionally, when your grandparents bought their first home, it was probably right around the Great Depression, or they were still hearing family stories about the Great Depression. Growing up, all your grandparents would hear was how during the Great Depression, the banks could just come and demand payment for your home. If you couldn't pay up, they could immediately foreclose on your house.

Those financially jarring stories were true; almost all loans before the Great Depression were callable. If the bank got into trouble, or if they thought you were in trouble, they could call the note. This was true even if your payments had always been on time.

When I think of this period in banking, I always remember the movie *It's a Wonderful Life* starring James Stewart as Mr. Bailey. James Stewart's on-screen nemesis was a crotchety old banker by the name of Mr. Potter. Potter takes over the town by the use of these demand notes; at least he would have if he could only get rid of that pesky Bailey Building and Loan Association.

Thank goodness the rules have changed! The odds of having a callable mortgage are just about nonexistent. But, for your grandparents, the 30-year, non-callable mortgage must have been a dream come true.

So picture your grandparents giving your parents advice. For the first time, there was the option of locking in your payment and, as long as you made it, the banks could never come and take your home. For your elders, with their experiences and losses during the Great Depression, don't you think they would have strongly encouraged that loan option? And since your parents have probably not had any experience with any other type of mortgage, they are just passing that family message down to you.

The reality is that a 30-year mortgage is great if you plan on owning a home for the full 30 years. If you don't, why pay a higher interest rate for the right to live there for 30 years? That's a little like paying for a hotel room for a month when you know you are going to stay there a week.

"The reality is that a 30-year mortgage is great if you plan on owning a home for the full 30 years. If you don't, why pay a

higher interest rate for the right to live there for 30 years?"

It never fails to amaze me when someone comes in and asks about a 30-year mortgage and then proceeds to tell me that within five years, they will move. Why would you want to voluntarily give more money to the bank?

15-year

The 15-year fixed works the same as the 30-year with the obvious exception that it lasts only 15 years. The good news is that if you stick with it, you will have your home fully paid off in 15 years. So, if you plan on being in a home for 15 years and can afford the higher payment, it is an option that you should consider.

However, if you plan on moving sooner, why spend the extra money?

One of the biggest points of confusion for people opting for the 15-year mortgage is that since they feel they are investing in their homes, they think their homes will somehow appreciate faster. Does the size of your mortgage impact whether your home appreciates? Not even a single penny. Think of it this way: If you buy a $500,000 home with no mortgage and, in one year, it appreciates by 5 percent, your net worth will increase by $25,000.

$500,000 x .05 = $25,000

On the other hand, if you purchase the same home, but this time it has a $500,000 mortgage - leaving you without a single cent in equity - will that impact the amount it appreciates? Not at all. The house would appreciate at the same rate - 5 percent - regardless. So in one year, the $500,000 house would still gain 5 percent and become a $525,000 home with a net increase of $25,000. The remaining balance on your mortgage in no way impacts the appreciation of your home.

$500,000 x .05 = $25,000 (The same exact calculation as above.)

In almost all situations, the buyer does not care about how much *you owe;* they care about how much *they will owe* when they buy the home. At this point, you probably are saying, "Yes, but on one house I owe $500,000, and I own another house free and clear. So isn't that a better situation?"

Well, to have a paid-off house, the money had to come from somewhere - so you either saved it or inherited it. Let's take the quicker approach and go with the inheritance. Picture yourself sitting in your brand-new home, which you just purchased with a mortgage with no money down for $500,000. To your great shock and amazement, you find out that your Great Aunt Bertie has left you $500,000. You immediately run to the bank and deposit it in your checking account and, for the first time in your life, you open your statement and find a balance of $500,000.

But now you have a decision to make. Do you pay off the $500,000 mortgage you owe on your brand-new home? Or invest the $500,000 for the future?

If you pay off the home, you save the mortgage expense minus the tax write-off. But the money isn't making you anything; again, the house appreciates whether you owe money on it or not. Your other choice is to invest the $500,000, but then you would still have to pay the mortgage expense net of the tax savings.

Which is best?

The question is: Does the return on the $500,000 that you have invested exceed the cost of interest minus any potential tax savings you may receive from the mortgage interest exemption?

If you purchase equities and, over the long run, your return on those investments is greater than your interest-rate costs, you win. If you assume an average 30-year stock market cycle - with S&P 500-like returns - this could easily mean $200,000 to almost $1,000,000 extra over 30 years (assuming a compounded annual rate of return of 5.51%). If, instead of investing in equities, you put the money into a savings account earning 1 percent, you are on the wrong end of the transaction and it could cost you the opportunity of earning hundreds of thousands of dollars had you invested in higher-earning assets.

For many people, this opportunity to make money using other people's money - is one of the fastest ways to gain real wealth. And there have been entire books written on the subject. Again, see *Missed Fortune* or, for a shorter rendition, look on the web for Ric Edelman's article "11 Great Reasons to Carry a Big, Long Mortgage."

In short, if you can both get a better return and protect the assets from creditors, then it is probably worth taking a look at.

"So, if you plan on being in a home for 15 years and can afford the higher payment, it is an option that you should consider."

Interest-only

Interest-only mortgages are exactly what they sound like. You make a payment, normally monthly, and your balance never goes down. Borrow $500,000 and 10 years later, you still owe $500,000.

Why would you ever do this?

One reason is that you do not plan on staying in the home long enough to pay it off anyway. A second reason is that you assume, over the next 30 years, that you will be able to earn more investing over and beyond what interest the bank is charging you net of any tax.

Let's look at the following example. Let's assume again that we are refinancing a $500,000 mortgage with a rate of 6.5

percent on a 30-year fixed, rate-amortized schedule. Your monthly payments will be $3,160 a month. At the end of 30 years, your house will be paid off.

30 years fixed rate = one home free and clear
(Which sounds good.)

If instead we look at the interest-only option, assuming the same 6.5 percent rate, your monthly note would drop to $2,709 per month allowing you to invest roughly $450 per month. Thirty years of investing $450 a month, at an assumed 8 percent net rate of return, amounts to $670,000. Which means you could not only pay off the $500,000, but also pocket an extra $170,000.

30 years of investing the difference at 8 percent

$670,000 - $500,000 = $170,000 plus one home free and clear
(Which sounds even better.)

Not bad. Especially when you consider that your assets would probably be more liquid in investments than they would be in your home. Don't forget that for most Americans, the spread is even better because I did not include any of the tax savings.

But let me be clear: *You should only do this if you are working with a professional and are being extremely careful.* You need to both understand the risk you are taking and make certain that you are going to save and not spend the difference. Otherwise, you just end up with one big, fat mortgage 30 years later, and no other investments to show for it.

ARMs

Adjustable-rate mortgages (ARMs) come in two flavors: interest-only and amortized. The only difference is self-explanatory. With a fixed-rate mortgage, your rate and your payment stay the same throughout the period of your loan. With an interest-only, your rate will fluctuate at regular intervals. These intervals range from 30 days to several years based on the prevailing rates when your lock- in period is up. ARMs normally offer lower rates at the point of inception than fixed rates because you are taking the interest rate risk instead of the bank.

"Adjustable-rate mortgages (ARMs) come in two flavors: interest-only and amortized."

To me, ARMs are one of the most dangerous types of loans because if rates go up dramatically, your mortgage payment goes up right along with them. If you have a floating, 30-day lock then your mortgage payment could literally go up every 30 days and if you have a five-year lock, it could go up at the end of the five-year term. Most people don't have room in their budgets for dramatic fluctuations.

"ARMs normally offer lower rates at the point of inception than fixed rates because you are taking the interest rate risk instead of the bank."

One way to counteract this fluctuation is to save the difference between the fixed- and adjustable-rate mortgages. On the day you are set to lock in a mortgage rate, get the rate for the 30-year fixed and the ARM you are considering and then save the difference between the two.

By saving money this way, you can then use a portion of the proceeds to pay for the increase in your note if your ARM ever goes above the fixed rate you were initially offered. The goal would be to have either a large lump sum from the invested difference to pay down your mortgage in order to lower your payment, or you could keep the money in reserve and draw from it, as needed, to cover the increase in your mortgage payments. If you do the latter, then even if rates increase, you may have a pool of money left over after completing all of your mortgage payments.

Although I have mentioned that ARMs are one of the most dangerous types of mortgages, they can also be one of the most efficient. The trick to taking advantage of the lower rates is locking the interest rate in for the period of time you plan on owning the house, and then add a couple of years extra, just in case you do not move as quickly as you had originally planned.

In this example, let's say you plan on living in your home for five years and then moving to a larger home as your family grows. Instead of locking in a rate for 30 years, you lock in your rate for seven years. The first five years are the years you plan on staying in the home and the extra two years allow you to ride out market conditions or just stay put because you love the home you are currently in.

Most people are shocked at how much this simple technique could save them. If there is just a one percent difference between the ARM and the 30-year fixed mortgage - and your mortgage is $500,000 - that is $5,000 per year that you could save. If you lived in the home for just five years and you left the $5,000 per year in your checking account - not earning a single penny - you would still end up with $25,000. If, at that point, you woke up and invested it in an average mutual fund for 20 years that earned 10 percent, it would amount to over $400,000.

It is the little things that keep most people from ending up with the wealth they have dreamed of.

"On the day you are set to lock in a mortgage rate, get the rate for the 30-year fixed and the ARM you are considering and then save the difference between the two."

My recommendation is that you take a serious look at the ARM and if you can be disciplined enough to save the difference, go for it. Just make sure you can either handle the swing in payments or lock in the rate for the period of time you plan on staying in the home - plus a couple of extra years for padding.

If you think there is any chance that you would just spend the interest savings, or that this may be the home you spend the rest of your life in, then go ahead and do a fixed mortgage. Remember, it's better having a paid-off home in 30 years than having an interest-only note and no savings.

One last note of caution: rates can and do swing. This year's six percent interest rate can be next year's 12 percent. If all you have is an interest-only mortgage with no rate lock, then your payments could double right along with the rates. So do the math or talk to a professional, but make sure you can handle the top mortgage rate stipulated in the contract. Whether that means you move to another home or find the cash flow for that higher mortgage payment, just be prepared and don't get in over your head. Remember anytime you choose an ARM, you always have to be prepared to make a change because your rate will adjust (as implied by the name) whether you like it or not.

"It is the little things that keep most people from ending up with the wealth they have dreamed of."

Law #4: Only furnish what you can afford

Picture yourself shopping online for that first home. You find one and call your agent to arrange the walk-through. You can't believe your luck! It is just what you always wanted. But you manage to show great restraint, great negotiating skills and get the owner to agree to terms that work for your budget. You fly through the process of getting the mortgage because you have already gotten pre-approved and have "Lived the Life" so you know you can afford it.

Many folks do a great job with this, only to fall victim to the fact that their beautiful new home has no furniture. My experience is that people pay between $5,000 and $10,000 per room for furniture and decorations. I used to think that those numbers were ridiculous, and if my wife asks me, they still are. However, many of my clients can easily reach the $10,000 mark. Several have spent that much just on the couch.

Cash or finance

If you missed my previous tirade about consumer debt, here it is again. Credit cards are dangerous! One of my favorite pearls of wisdom with regard to debt is from Solomon in

Proverbs 22:7, "The rich rules over the poor, And the borrower becomes the lender's slave." That is tough language, and granted I am no theologian, but just think about what that means.

People with assets have control (e.g., business owners, professionals, and politicians). During biblical times, if you couldn't pay your bills, you literally could become a slave to your lender. So from that perspective, it wasn't really a statement of theology – it was a warning. In other words, you better have a darn good reason for not being able to service your debts because until you pay your debt, you are a slave to the holder of that debt (your creditor).

Fortunately, in modern times, if you are late with your credit card bill, your credit card company cannot quite go to those extremes. But think about it, if your entire income goes to pay interest, have things really changed that much over the millennium? And if you miss a couple of payments, the bill collectors will certainly make you feel like a criminal.

If you cannot pay with cash, **don't** buy it, even if they are advertising zero percent interest for the next 15 years. Remember, there is always a catch. They are running a business, so they won't make offers that don't benefit them.

So, what do you do?

Beg, Borrow, & Steal

You probably need to be a little creative. Wait to furnish a room until you have the money, buy used, borrow from friends, or raid your parents' home. Any of these ideas work and can save you a small fortune.

If you know your parents have several items that you would like to have,_-and that you may inherit, now may be a good time to have that discussion. Yes, it is uncomfortable, but if there ever was a rational time to broach this topic, now is it. The reasons are pretty clear.

"If you know your parents have several items that you would like to have, and that you may inherit, now may be a good time to have that discussion."

First, it saves you money, which puts you in a better financial position. This will make both you and them happy. Second, it will allow them to see you enjoy the furniture in their lifetimes. Finally, and possibly most importantly, it will keep some of those precious heirlooms from being auctioned. One of the more common reasons for auctions or estate sales today is that the inheritors are already settled and do not have the room for their parents' family treasures. If certain pieces of furniture could be transferred from one generation to the next earlier in life, a lot fewer pieces would make it to auction.

In many situations, this may not work. But in many, it will. Regardless, it never hurts to ask.

Law #5: Go green

You can potentially save a bundle on utility bills and be gentler on the planet by considering "green" alternatives as you begin maintaining your home. Right off the bat, you may want to have the ducts tested for leaks. Some experts say that properly sealing them is the best energy upgrade you can make. However, don't try to do it with duct tape since that often doesn't work well. I've been told that the best thing to use is something called Mastic.

"You can potentially save a bundle on utility bills and be gentler on the planet by considering "green" alternatives as you begin the maintenance your home."

Need better insulation? You might be able to just drill holes into the drywall, add spray-foam insulation, seal the holes and repaint the walls. (Of course, get an expert evaluation first.) This can potentially make the house more energy-efficient and quieter. Insulating a home this way will often enable you to install smaller heating and air conditioning units.

Your home should have been tested for radon during the inspection. Should you have an issue with this, now is the time to address it. And to further optimize indoor air quality, keep an eye out for green alternatives when buying carpeting, stains, sealants, cleaning supplies and furniture; and use air filters, dehumidifiers and window exhaust fans to draw stale air out of your home, and bring fresh air in.

Other green items you might consider include a gray water system, Energy Star appliances, a geothermal heat pump, no- and low-VOC paint, low-e windows, low-flow faucets, rainwater barrels, energy-efficient washing machines and dryers and solar water heating, which generally costs a few thousand dollars.

Should you be interested in building green, you will probably become acquainted with the word "LEED." LEED is a U.S. Green Building Council program and stands for Leadership in Energy and Environmental Design. With LEED, the homebuilding process is heavily scrutinized and certification is awarded at three different levels: silver, gold and platinum.

LEED for Homes is a relatively new program, dating back seven years and regional green building programs are also prevalent. I'm told that a few of a the leading ones include the EarthCraft House program in Atlanta, Georgia; Austin Energy Green Building in Austin, Texas; and Built Green in Colorado. With any program, it's very important to look into who is doing the certification and what a builder must do to have a home certified. Independent third-party certification will ensure the quality of the construction much more than self-certification; the latter simply requires a builder to check off what has been done.

Some green building programs, like LEED and EarthCraft House, also certify renovation work. Other popular trends in green building include the incorporation of smart technologies (e.g., home automation systems, which can sometimes detail energy usage throughout the home). And masonry homes have been getting a lot of buzz in recent years; particularly, insulated concrete forms (ICFs), which are masonry-like building materials that optimize insulation, longevity and minimize construction waste.

Chapter 7

How to Buy Your First Car

The last big-ticket item that people purchase around the same time as their first home is their first car.

New vs. Used

The most common question is whether to buy new or used. If we look at some simple math, the answer is pretty obvious. Everyone, or at least almost everyone, has heard that a car drops in value as quickly as you drive it off the lot. With most cars, this depreciation is actually in the range of 20 percent.

What most people don't realize is that if you take care of the car, the best time to sell it is not when the wheels are about to fall off, but just before the car turns five. For many people, the difference between a car that is one or two years old isn't that great. However, when a car is over five years of age, it is no longer considered a late-model car. Odds are that in that five-year period, even body styles will have changed; so, not only is it older, but it doesn't even look like one of the newer models.

"What most people don't realize is that if you take care of the car, the best time to sell it is not when the wheels are about to fall off, but just before the car turns five."

Late-model cars have several things that detract from their value. First, they normally have higher financing costs. Add in more mileage, and newer models sitting in showrooms, and you can begin to understand why they might depreciate faster for a couple of years.

The Decision

Okay, you have probably already admitted to yourself that you need to be shopping for a used car rather than a new car. But that still leaves a decision. Are you shopping for the lightly used, late-model vehicle that is a little more fashionable (and by that I mean a little more expensive)? Or something a little older?

Remember my warning about that burst of depreciation right around the five-year mark?

Well, that makes those cars that are seven-plus years old, with a little higher mileage and older body styles, a bargain. They potentially have a few more mechanical problems than a newer model, but the lower cost can more than make up for it. Remember most of today's cars can easily run between 150,000 and 200,000 miles before there are serious mechanical issues.

Look at your budget and at what you want to buy. If you are desperate for that new car look and can afford it, then buy a one-year-old car and replace it every four to five years. If you just do this, you are ahead of the average consumer.

However, if you want the absolute best deal, you need to find a car that has just undergone a major body style change, and look for a low mileage version of the previous body style - preferably in the four- to six-year time frame. The body style change results in faster depreciation of the older model, which means you get a bargain.

"However, if you want the absolute best deal, you need to find a car that has just undergone a major body style change, and look for a low mileage version of the previous body style -

preferably in the four- to six-year time frame."

Even if you choose not to go with the older models and instead stick with the late-model car that you sell by year five, the savings can be enormous. Let's assume you are a two-car family that replaces each car every five years. You would end up with roughly $40,000 in savings between just your 20th and 30th birthdays. If you then invest that $40,000 until your retirement, at age 65, assuming a 10 percent return over 35 years, you would have approximately $1,124,097 more saved for retirement.

How many people realize that buying a couple of new cars in their 20s could have cost them over $1 million in retirement? And if you are willing to give up a couple of those prestige points and drive the slightly older body style that is four-plus years old, you can probably double your savings.

"How many people realize that buying a couple of new cars in their 20s could have cost them over $1 million in retirement?"

Financing, Leasing, Cash?

Which do you choose?

Hopefully I have convinced you that purchasing a car that is at least one year old (and being a millionaire!) is better than having a brand-new car and being poor in retirement.

Next, comes the question of paying for it.

In today's world you can still lease, finance, or pay cash. And depending upon your situation, any of the three may work.

First let's look at the cash option. Generally speaking, and in a perfect world, this is the best. The fact is that you should not buy a car until you can pay cash for it. In other words, you should keep driving your old car until you have cash to pay for that new car.

"The fact is that you should not buy a car until you can pay cash for it."

However, having worked with young professionals, I know the odds of you pulling up to your new office in a jalopy are slim!

Anyway, even if you have the cash to pay for the car, always compare all three options and get a quote for each. Many times, especially at a dealership, they may offer you different prices or deals based upon your financing choice. So check that first.

Next, see if they are running any specials on interest. Currently, I am hearing about "certified used car financing" for around one percent. You can get a CD earning around five percent (this is an example of how much rates can change over time in 2006 these numbers were accurate in 2014 you would be happy to get a 1% CD – who knows what they will be by the time you read this book). Even if you take taxes into consideration, you will probably net somewhere between two and three percent on your balance. It may not sound like much, but over time, it can really add up.

The factors to look at when you decide between leasing and normal financing are a little more complicated. But unless you are going to trade your car in every two or three years, with very low mileage, you probably do not have a chance of winning with leasing; that is, unless you are a small business and can take advantage of the tax write-offs. Even in this situation, most accountants will tell you it is the worst of your three options.

"But unless you are going to trade your car in every two or three years, with very low mileage, you probably do not have a chance of winning with leasing; that is, unless you are a small business and can take advantage of the tax write-offs."

The recommendations:

1. Buy used.
2. Compare all three options (i.e., cash, loan and lease).
3. Whenever possible, pay CASH!!
4. Always pay one car off before purchasing your next one.

Chapter 8

How to Stay Safe Online

It's a sign of the times that I now ask my clients to attend an annual seminar with an FBI agent to stay safe online. Special Agent to the FBI "Ryan Johnson" (the agent's true name has been altered to protect his identity) tells them how to protect their accounts. He emphasizes that cybercrime is quickly becoming the most pervasive type of crime in the United States. "It's estimated that for the FBI, cybercrime will probably be our #1 priority in a few years," Ryan says. Most cases lead overseas, there are approximately 16,000 new viruses manufactured every day and in 2010, identity thieves cost individuals approximately $5 billion and businesses $48 billion nationwide.

"It's estimated that for the FBI, cybercrime will probably be our #1 priority in a few years ..."

Ryan tells my clients that although the Internet is a key part of financial management nowadays, all financial transactions should really be done on a separate computer. "Probably the best way to do online banking is from a standalone computer," he says. "Don't download email on that computer; don't surf online. Only go to your bank's website and then close it out. And it should have a good firewall and the anti-virus should be constantly updated."

Ryan advises them that they can also create a virtual machine on their primary computers with special software. So you essentially install a separate operating system on that computer. He says that Macs are still safer than PCs because they have been such a low percentage of the marketshare, but that's quickly changing.

"We're seeing malware now written specifically for Macs," he tells me. "But in general, PC users are the low-hanging fruit." The greatest vulnerability is getting a phishing email, clicking on it, and getting a keylogger. At that stage, user names and passwords can be easily recovered by the keylogging software.

He also tells my clients that passwords:

➢ should be very complex,
➢ changed every three months,
➢ should be six or more characters with uppercase, lowercase and special characters and numbers,

> ➤ and he recommends recording them in a paper address book, which should be kept within a safe in your home.

Of course, make sure that your anti-virus software is up to date and download software patches as they become available. In terms of Wi-Fi, Ryan recommends never doing financial transactions in a public setting, even with password-protected Wi-Fi. But if you do, use your credit card; never use your debit card.

Wi-Fi

Ryan tells me that whether you use a hotspot or personal Wi-Fi, the key again is having a strong password. "A lot of people don't set passwords on those. And once you get onto that, you can easily get into someone's computer with simple vulnerabilities like not keeping software patches updated."

Wi-Fi has gotten a lot better, but if you are using Wi-Fi, it should be password-protected with at least WPA protection, he says. "It will ask you when you set up your router, what sort of authentication you want and WPA is the one you want to select. It can be hacked, but it takes time. The hackers are going to have to be within wireless range of your router and they are going to have to grab a lot of packets of data in order to eventually hack that password. So it's not really practical."

There's a feature in mobile devices that will search for open wireless devices and Ryan recommends shutting it off "So that you don't automatically join up to a network that you don't want to be on. You unintentionally open yourself up to intrusions in your phone and can make yourself a wireless access point as well."

Also, consider disabling location services on your cellphone as this enables geotagging. "Geotagging is when someone will take a picture with his or her smartphone and it will record the latitude and longitude in the properties of the picture. When it's uploaded to Facebook, people can download the information and see exactly where you are," Ryan explains.

"This is what I tell people: Don't become the low-hanging fruit. If you are surfing the web, reading email, clicking on everything that has an attachment, and spending time on Facebook, then you become very vulnerable. If you are doing the basic things like only friending people you know for sure on Facebook, and when you get an email with an attachment and have no idea who it's from, you delete it, you make it a lot harder," Ryan says.

"Don't become the low-hanging fruit. If you are surfing the web, reading email, clicking on everything that has an attachment, and spending time on Facebook, then you become very vulnerable."

"Better yet is when your firewall, anti-virus, and operating system are up-to-date, you make it even harder. And if you use a whole separate computer for your banking only and don't surf the web, the bad guys will just go on to the easier people. Only do your banking on that computer. Alternatively, you can set up multiple virtual machines and do separate things on each one. But that can get expensive. "

Staying Safe on the Road

Particularly if you need to send sensitive data while on the road, consider using encrypted email, establishing a virtual-private network, storing data on encrypted thumb drives with locks, using a prepaid credit card for online transactions and ensuring you've got your mobile devices set to destroy their data after 10 or so password attempts.

"Particularly if you need to send sensitive data while on the road, consider using encrypted email, establishing a virtual-private network, storing data on encrypted thumb drives with locks, using a prepaid credit card for online transactions and ensuring you've got your mobile devices set to destroy their data after 10 or so password attempts."

"In general, if you are traveling overseas, don't carry confidential and personal data on your computer," Ryan tells me. "For information you do have on your computer, I recommend that you have full-disk encryption. That protects a lot of your files. It's not 100 percent, but it's very difficult for someone to get at that information if the hard drive is copied or stolen. Also, there are certain countries requiring extra care."

My own phone was hacked overseas a couple of years ago. My travel was part of the M.B.A. program at Vanderbilt University; we spoke with business owners and learned how to do business overseas. I had gotten a special, encrypted phone for work-related communications, but brought my personal phone as well. We had been forewarned about visiting a certain electronics firm and as soon as we stepped onto the property, my phone quit taking pictures. I didn't even notice it immediately. My camera was restored upon leaving the property, but my photos had been slightly reshuffled.

Also, newer passports, along with some driver's licenses and credit cards, have chips embedded in them, and can transmit your data to anyone with commonplace RFID readers. So consider using an RFID-blocking passport case for your passport, credit cards and driver's license. Many people also don't know that they should consider getting a second passport for some travel. It can expedite visa processing and permit travel to countries at odds with each other.

"Also, strongly consider getting an RFID-blocking passport case for your

passport, credit cards and driver's license. That's because newer passports, along with some driver's licenses and credit cards, have chips embedded in them, and can transmit your data to anyone with commonplace RFID readers."

Protecting Your Online Identity

The societal trend, today, is often towards greater online notoriety. This can make you quite vulnerable in many ways. A typical case of identity theft, for example, can take 180 days to resolve so it's important to start weighing the risks and benefits of your activities online. Also, as you progress in your career, you'll increasingly find people pursuing online *anonymity* as much as possible. This doesn't necessarily mean going cold turkey on the social media, but you should be extremely careful.

"A typical case of identity theft ... can take 180 days to resolve ..."

You can begin protecting yourself by limiting your social networks and the information you share publicly. Also, refrain from giving out any unnecessary data at stores and elsewhere (particularly your social security number) and do web searches using your name and try to delete any unnecessary information online. You'll find that there are plenty of websites with data on you, like your name, age, relatives, and location. Their privacy pages will guide you in "opting out." Some top sites, according to ZDNet, include:

- Intellius.com
- PeopleFinders.com
- Peekyou.com
- Spokeo.com
- BeenVerified.com
- MyLife.com
- PeopleLookUp.com
- PeopleSmart.com
- Radaris.com
- Spoke.com
- USA-People-Search.com
- Zabasearch.com
- USSearch.com
- Whitepages.com

"It's so important to monitor and eliminate what's on these people-search sites about you," says Leslie Holoweiko Hobbs,

Public Relations Director at Reputation.com. "These are a reflection of the data that's getting bought and sold and bought again - by people you don't know for purposes you'll never know. It's becoming increasingly apparent that the innocuous personal details about you reveal so much in aggregate. That's helpful information for identity thieves, stalkers, retailers, and more. It's also unclear how this data could be used in the future - could profiles be used to determine your health or credit-worthiness?

So treat the Internet like a virtual garden by weeding consistently, staying educated, and being mindful of the image you are projecting out into the world.

Chapter 9

Get a Plan – Get an Advisor – Do Not Practice on Yourself

So if you have not already done so, get a plan and get it professionally done. If you are a DIYer, then I recommend working with a fee-based planner who can do a solid, unbiased job and confirm your decisions, or at least help you get on the right path before it is too late.

Once you have decided how to model your investment plan, it is also important to understand how those models work. The first method, and still the most common, is what I refer to as the "Straight-Line Model." The line is not normally straight, but rather has a generally smooth curve (hopefully up). The reason I refer to this model as the straight-line method is that if you look at what it assumes the returns on the portfolio are going to be, it is a perfectly straight line.

Let's say the planner assumes that you are going to average eight percent. So, every year your return will be eight percent; never a better year, never a worse year. Well, that is great if the market outperforms year after year, but what if we have a significant correction and your portfolio is down? Most people do not realize how difficult it is to make up for a negative year in their portfolios until it happens.

Monte Carlo is the name of the method I personally prefer, although I generally run both models for my clients. The reason I like Monte Carlo better is that it bases its model on actual market performance. Additionally, instead of saying everything is good or everything is bad, it gives probabilities of where you will be with your portfolio, assuming the same asset allocation in the future.

In other words, it will say there is a 50 percent chance you will be over this number, an 80 percent chance you will be over that number, and a 95 percent chance that you will have some number on an annual basis. In this way, every year you can track where you are in the range and, to some degree, you can also judge what your advisor is doing on your behalf against long-term statistical odds. For example, if your adviser does not hit the number, year after year, it might be time to look for a new advisor. Also, if your advisor can't tell you the difference between a straight-line calculation and a Monte Carlo, trade your advisor in.

Be Conservative – Diversify – Diversify – Diversify.

You can potentially make more money by selecting a single asset, or even a single asset class, but this is not the time to do it. When you are at this stage, you are at the point where a mistake can be fatal; at least financially.

If your portfolio was properly diversified, you may have not been excited about the recent market correction but you were probably okay. If you were not well diversified, however, then you could have lost a significant portion of your investments at just about the time you planned on taking withdrawals.

When I had only been in the business a couple of years, I received a referral from one of my clients. It was in the late 1990s and the new client had paid me a $2,500 retainer to look over his situation. Over 90 percent of this gentleman's net worth was in one stock. Frankly, it had made him rich; he was planning on purchasing a home in California and living on Easy Street for the rest of his life.

I almost begged the client to diversify. But I soon realized that there was nothing I could do for this gentleman, so I refunded him his retainer and referred him to a broker I knew. It was only a little under two years later that this man's house of cards came crashing down.

To this day I am sad because I feel I failed this gentleman. An older advisor gave me an expression, though, that I will also always remember: you cannot care more about a client than they care about themselves. For that reason, I have chosen to work with people who care about themselves (and those around them) and who also understand that too much of a good thing is never good.

So update your plan every year because if you make an error now, you will still probably have time to play catch-up. Also, greed will get you; it is not a question of if, it is a question of when. And diversify, diversify and diversify.

Outro

You have a wonderful future ahead of you. There will be many challenges, plenty of opportunities and your focus should always be on building, building, building – your portfolio, your relationships, your living situation. That doesn't always mean buying a bigger and bigger home. It does mean making your lifestyle work for the unique needs of you and your family.

Stressors can come at us from every angle and the fewer you have, on a daily basis, the more happiness, peace of mind and goodness you will enjoy in your life. But the bottom line to all of this, as I said in the opening, money is merely a tool to make these things happen.

Manage it wisely so that you never have to experience it managing you.

Trey Smith, CFP®, CIMA, ChFC, CRPC

When selecting a financial advisor, you want someone with integrity, professionalism and experience. As your SunTrust Investment Services Private Financial Advisor, Trey Smith brings those qualities and many more, including insightful advice and in-depth knowledge in the following areas:

• Investment Management
• Financial Planning
• Estate Strategies and Wealth Preservation
• Retirement Planning
• Philanthropic Planning

Trey offers clients more than 10 years of investment experience. He works collaboratively with clients toassess their financial situation, goals and objectives, determines risk tolerance, and forms and executes an appropriate investment plan to obtain measurable results.

Trey, with the support of Financial Consultant Mat Tyndal, Investment Associate Alex Pittenger, and Administrative Associate Crystal Morgan, help clients make the most of the life they have by focusing on the goals they value most.

Trey believes that only through expanding your knowledge base can you better assess the needs of theclient and the ever changing market and economy. For this reason, in addition to his B.A. in Economicsfrom the University of Illinois and his CFP, ChFC, CRPC certifications, he has recently completed the Executive MBA program at Vanderbilt University.

Trey has been active in several community organizations including but not limited to the West Nashville Sports League where he helped coach a basketball team, and has been one of the acting class chair for Harding Academy's annual fund. Trey is also a member of the Financial Planning Association. In addition to having published several articles, Trey has been asked to speak on behalf of the Aquinas College's Lecture series and for the Tennessee Independent College and Universities Association.

In his spare time, Trey enjoys photography and spending time with his family. He and his wife, Dianne, have 2 daughters, Katelyn and Larissa.

The opinions and information contained herein have been obtained or derived from sources believed to be reliable, but SunTrust Investment Services, Inc. (STIS) makes no representation or guarantee as to their timeliness, accuracy or completeness or for their fitness for any particular purpose. The information contained herein does not purport to be a complete analysis of any security, company, or industry involved. This material is not be construed as an offer to sell or a solicitation of an offer to buy any security. The information and material presented herein are for general information only and do not specifically address individual investment objectives, financial situations or the particular needs of any specific person who may *receive this book. Investing in any security or investment strategies discussed herein may not be suitable for you, and you may want to consult a financial advisor. Nothing in this material constitutes individual investment, legal or tax advice. Investments involve risk and an investor may incur either profits or losses. Past performance should not be taken as an indication or guarantee of future performance*

Investment and Insurance Products:
•Are not FDIC or any other Government Agency Insured•Are not Bank Guaranteed •May Lose Value

Securities, insurance (including annuities) and other investment products and services are offered by SunTrust Investment Services, Inc., an SEC registered investment adviser and broker-dealer affiliate of SunTrust Banks, Inc., member FINRA, SIPC, and a licensed insurance agency.

The Forms

The following and final section of the book includes some basic forms that could come in handy throughout your life. Some you will need to keep in your personal file and some are meant to be kept with the people in your life you trust or are helping you in a specific situation.

In this new world of technology the act of filling out forms may seem antiquated but the reality is this is the best way to share information in an easy to find format. For example you may thing that all of your advisors will be on your phone contact list so why would you want to make a separate list – the answer is simple and straightforward: if you are like me, you have hundreds of names in your contact list and they are not subdivided by how they relate to you. You know who is who but no one else would be able to figure who is a friend who happens to be a Doctor and who is your actual Doctor.

The forms will be grouped in sections based on how you might use them (although some forms may be used multiple times)

If you would prefer to have these forms in an electronic format I will be happy to forward them to you – just e-mail me at **Trey.Smith@SunTrust.com** with "FORMS" in the subject line. That you way you can fill them out and forward them electronically rather than having to print and scan each one.

"For Your Files" and is only meant to seen by you and potentially the person you trust if you were incapacitated.

- Personal Advisor Contact List
- Emergency Contact Information
- Important Dates
- Personal Medical History
- Physician's Contact List
- Family Information
- Bank Account Summary
- Household Item Location List
- Personal Advisor Contact List

For your Emergency Contact

- Physician Contact List
- Emergency Contact Information
- Household Item Location List

Travel

- For your eyes only
  - Personal Medical History (Just in case)
  - Physician's Contact List
  - Travel Packing List
  - Travel Itinerary
  - Emergency Contact Information
- To be shared with trusted person\House\Pet Sitter
  - Emergency Contact List
  - Travel Itinerary
  - Household Items Location List
  - Emergency Contact Information

Financial Advisors

- Personal Advisor Contact List
- Bank Account Summary
- Family Information

Personal Advisor Contact List

Financial Advisor:
Name: _____ Firm: _____
Phone: _____ Email: _____
Address: _____

Accountant:
Name: _____ Firm: _____
Phone: _____ Email: _____
Address: _____

Attorney:
Name: _____ Firm: _____
Phone: _____ Email: _____
Address: _____

Banking Advisor:
Name: _____ Firm: _____
Phone: _____ Email: _____
Address: _____

Banking Advisor:
Name: _____ Firm: _____
Phone: _____ Email: _____
Address: _____

Insurance Agent:
Name: _____ Firm: _____
Phone: _____ Email: _____
Address: _____

Insurance Agent:
Name: _____ Firm: _____
Phone: _____ Email: _____
Address: _____

Realtor:
Name: _____ Firm: _____
Phone: _____ Email: _____
Address: _____

Primary Physician:
Name: _____ Firm: _____
Phone: _____ Email: _____
Address: _____

Other Advisor:
Name: _____ Firm: _____
Phone: _____ Email: _____
Address: _____

Emergency Contact Information

Home Address: _____

City: _____ St: _____ Zip: _____

Home Phone(s): _____, _____, _____

Mobile Phone(s): _____, _____, _____

Fire Department: _____ **Police Department:** _____
Ambulance: _____ **Poison Control:** _____
Home Alarm Co.: _____ **Alarm Code:** _____

Closest Hospital: _____ **Phone:** _____
Address: _____
Primary Doctor: _____ **Phone:** _____
Veterinarian: _____ **Phone:** _____
Pharmacy: _____ **Phone:** _____

Emg. Conatct: _____ **Relationship:** _____
Address: _____
Primary Phone: _____ Alternate Phone: _____

Alternate #1: _____ **Relationship:** _____
Address: _____
Primary Phone: _____ Alternate Phone: _____

Alternate #2: _____ **Relationship:** _____
Address: _____
Primary Phone: _____ Alternate Phone: _____

Attorney: _____ **Relationship:** _____
Address: _____
Primary Phone: _____ Alternate Phone: _____

Accountant: _____ **Firm:** _____
Address: _____
Primary Phone: _____ Alternate Phone: _____

Fin. Advisor: _____ **Manager:** _____
Address: _____
Primary Phone: _____ Alternate Phone: _____

Employer: _____ **Manager:** _____
Address: _____
Primary Phone: _____ Alternate Phone: _____

Important Dates

January:
   Date: _____ Event: _____   Date: _____ Event: _____
   Date: _____ Event: _____   Date: _____ Event: _____
   Date: _____ Event: _____   Date: _____ Event: _____

February:
   Date: _____ Event: _____   Date: _____ Event: _____
   Date: _____ Event: _____   Date: _____ Event: _____
   Date: _____ Event: _____   Date: _____ Event: _____

March:
   Date: _____ Event: _____   Date: _____ Event: _____
   Date: _____ Event: _____   Date: _____ Event: _____
   Date: _____ Event: _____   Date: _____ Event: _____

April:
   Date: _____ Event: _____   Date: _____ Event: _____
   Date: _____ Event: _____   Date: _____ Event: _____
   Date: _____ Event: _____   Date: _____ Event: _____

May:
   Date: _____ Event: _____   Date: _____ Event: _____
   Date: _____ Event: _____   Date: _____ Event: _____
   Date: _____ Event: _____   Date: _____ Event: _____

June:
   Date: _____ Event: _____   Date: _____ Event: _____
   Date: _____ Event: _____   Date: _____ Event: _____
   Date: _____ Event: _____   Date: _____ Event: _____

July:
   Date: _____ Event: _____   Date: _____ Event: _____
   Date: _____ Event: _____   Date: _____ Event: _____
   Date: _____ Event: _____   Date: _____ Event: _____

August:
   Date: _____ Event: _____   Date: _____ Event: _____
   Date: _____ Event: _____   Date: _____ Event: _____
   Date: _____ Event: _____   Date: _____ Event: _____

September:
   Date: _____ Event: _____   Date: _____ Event: _____
   Date: _____ Event: _____   Date: _____ Event: _____
   Date: _____ Event: _____   Date: _____ Event: _____

October:
   Date: _____ Event: _____   Date: _____ Event: _____
   Date: _____ Event: _____   Date: _____ Event: _____
   Date: _____ Event: _____   Date: _____ Event: _____

November:
   Date: _____ Event: _____   Date: _____ Event: _____
   Date: _____ Event: _____   Date: _____ Event: _____
   Date: _____ Event: _____   Date: _____ Event: _____

December:
   Date: _____ Event: _____   Date: _____ Event: _____
   Date: _____ Event: _____   Date: _____ Event: _____
   Date: _____ Event: _____   Date: _____ Event: _____

Important Dates

January:
Date: _____ Event: _____	Date: _____ Event: _____
Date: _____ Event: _____	Date: _____ Event: _____
Date: _____ Event: _____	Date: _____ Event: _____

February:
Date: _____ Event: _____	Date: _____ Event: _____
Date: _____ Event: _____	Date: _____ Event: _____
Date: _____ Event: _____	Date: _____ Event: _____

March:
Date: _____ Event: _____	Date: _____ Event: _____
Date: _____ Event: _____	Date: _____ Event: _____
Date: _____ Event: _____	Date: _____ Event: _____

April:
Date: _____ Event: _____	Date: _____ Event: _____
Date: _____ Event: _____	Date: _____ Event: _____
Date: _____ Event: _____	Date: _____ Event: _____

May:
Date: _____ Event: _____	Date: _____ Event: _____
Date: _____ Event: _____	Date: _____ Event: _____
Date: _____ Event: _____	Date: _____ Event: _____

June:
Date: _____ Event: _____	Date: _____ Event: _____
Date: _____ Event: _____	Date: _____ Event: _____
Date: _____ Event: _____	Date: _____ Event: _____

July:
Date: _____ Event: _____	Date: _____ Event: _____
Date: _____ Event: _____	Date: _____ Event: _____
Date: _____ Event: _____	Date: _____ Event: _____

August:
Date: _____ Event: _____	Date: _____ Event: _____
Date: _____ Event: _____	Date: _____ Event: _____
Date: _____ Event: _____	Date: _____ Event: _____

September:
Date: _____ Event: _____	Date: _____ Event: _____
Date: _____ Event: _____	Date: _____ Event: _____
Date: _____ Event: _____	Date: _____ Event: _____

October:
Date: _____ Event: _____	Date: _____ Event: _____
Date: _____ Event: _____	Date: _____ Event: _____
Date: _____ Event: _____	Date: _____ Event: _____

November:
Date: _____ Event: _____	Date: _____ Event: _____
Date: _____ Event: _____	Date: _____ Event: _____
Date: _____ Event: _____	Date: _____ Event: _____

December:
Date: _____ Event: _____	Date: _____ Event: _____
Date: _____ Event: _____	Date: _____ Event: _____
Date: _____ Event: _____	Date: _____ Event: _____

Personal Medical History

Personal Medical History

Full Legal Name: _____

Date of Birth: _____ Place of Birth: _____ Hospital: _____

Insurance Company: _____

Group Number: _____ Member Number: _____ Co-Pay: _____

Blood Type: _____ Allergies: _____

Emergency Contact #1: _____

Phone: _____ Fax: _____ Email: _____

Emergency Contact #2: _____

Phone: _____ Fax: _____ Email: _____

Primary Physician: _____

Hospital: _____

Phone: _____ Fax: _____ Email: _____

Immunization/Diseases	**Year**	**Immunizations/Diseases**	**Year**
Chicken Pox		Bleeding problems	
Diphtheria		Blood disease	
Hepatitis A / B		Diabetes	
HIB (or DPT + HIB)		Epilepsy	
HIV + or AIDS		Healing Problems	
Measles		Heart Disease	
Mumps		High blood pressure	
Pertussis		Kidney disorders	
Polio		Rheumatic fever	
Rubella		Respiratory fever	
Tetanus		Scarlet Fever	
Cancer (specify)		Other_____	

Previous Surgeries	**Date**	**Doctor**
_____	_____	_____
_____	_____	_____
_____	_____	_____
_____	_____	_____
_____	_____	_____

Current Medications:	**Dosage:**	**Prescribing Doctor:**
_____	_____	_____
_____	_____	_____
_____	_____	_____
_____	_____	_____
_____	_____	_____
_____	_____	_____
_____	_____	_____

Personal Medical History Cont.

Eyeglass prescriptions: _____

Previous Exams:

Date of last physical: _____
Date of last Blood Screening: _____
Date of last Dental Exam: _____
Date of last Eye Exam: _____

Other Notes:

_____
_____
_____
_____
_____
_____
_____
_____
_____
_____
_____
_____
_____
_____

Physician's Contact List

Primary Physician: _____   Hospital: _____
Phone: _____   Fax: _____
Address: _____

Pediatrician: _____   Hospital: _____
Phone: _____   Fax: _____
Address: _____

Cardiologist: _____   Hospital: _____
Phone: _____   Fax: _____
Address: _____

Dentist: _____   Hospital: _____
Phone: _____   Fax: _____
Address: _____

Orthodontist: _____   Hospital: _____
Phone: _____   Fax: _____
Address: _____

Ear, Nose, Throat Physician: _____   Hospital: _____
Phone: _____   Fax: _____
Address: _____

Internal Medicine Physician: _____   Hospital: _____
Phone: _____   Fax: _____
Address: _____

OBGYN Physician: _____   Hospital: _____
Phone: _____   Fax: _____
Address: _____

Oncologist: _____   Hospital: _____
Phone: _____   Fax: _____
Address: _____

Ophthalmologist: _____   Hospital: _____
Phone: _____   Fax: _____
Address: _____

Optometrist: _____   Hospital: _____
Phone: _____   Fax: _____
Address: _____

Physical Therapist: _____   Hospital: _____
Phone: _____   Fax: _____
Address: _____

Physician's Contact List Cont.

Orthopedic Specialist: _____ Hospital:

Phone: _____ Fax:

Address:

Surgeon: _____ Hospital:

Phone: _____ Fax:

Address:

Psychiatrist: _____ Hospital:

Phone: _____ Fax:

Address:

Other doctor: _____ Hospital:

Phone: _____ Fax:

Address:

Other doctor: _____ Hospital:

Phone: _____ Fax:

Address:

Other doctor: _____ Hospital:

Phone: _____ Fax:

Address:

Family Information

Name: _____ Birthday: _____
Phone: _____ Email Address: _____
Address: _____

Spouse: _____ Birthday: _____
Phone: _____ Email Address: _____
Address: _____

Child: _____ Birthday: _____
Phone: _____ Email Address: _____
Address: _____

Child: _____ Birthday: _____
Phone: _____ Email Address: _____
Address: _____

Child: _____ Birthday: _____
Phone: _____ Email Address: _____
Address: _____

Father: _____ Birthday: _____
Phone: _____ Email Address: _____
Address: _____

Mother: _____ Birthday: _____
Phone: _____ Email Address: _____
Address: _____

Father-In-Law: _____ Birthday: _____
Phone: _____ Email Address: _____
Address: _____

Mother-In-Law: _____ Birthday: _____
Phone: _____ Email Address: _____
Address: _____

Sibling: _____ Birthday: _____
Phone: _____ Email Address: _____
Address: _____

Sibling: _____ Birthday: _____
Phone: _____ Email Address: _____
Address: _____

Sibling: _____ Birthday: _____
Phone: _____ Email Address: _____
Address: _____

Sibling: _____ Birthday: _____
Phone: _____ Email Address: _____
Address: _____

Bank Account Summary

Bank: _____
Address: _____
Contact: _____ Phone: _____ Email: _____

Type:	Account Number:	Authorized Parties:	Checkbook Location:
Checking:	_____	_____	_____
Checking:	_____	_____	_____
Savings:	_____	_____	_____
Savings:	_____	_____	_____
Money Mkt:	_____	_____	_____

Bank: _____
Address: _____
Contact: _____ Phone: _____ Email: _____

Type:	Account Number:	Authorized Parties:	Checkbook Location:
Checking:	_____	_____	_____
Checking:	_____	_____	_____
Savings:	_____	_____	_____
Savings:	_____	_____	_____
Money Mkt:	_____	_____	_____

Bank: _____
Address: _____
Contact: _____ Phone: _____ Email: _____

Type:	Account Number:	Authorized Parties:	Checkbook Location:
Checking:	_____	_____	_____
Checking:	_____	_____	_____
Savings:	_____	_____	_____
Savings:	_____	_____	_____
Money Mkt:	_____	_____	_____

Household Item Location List

Burglary Alarm:

Location description for main keypad: _____

_____

Security code#: _____ Security Word/Phrase: _____

Carbon—Monoxide Detector Location(s):

Location #1 Description: _____
Location #2 Description: _____
* Spare Batteries for the Carbon-Monoxide Detectors are located: _____

_____ _____

Fire Detector Location(s):

Location #1 Description: _____
Location #2 Description: _____
Location #3 Description: _____
* Spare batteries for the Fire Detectors are located: _____

_____

Electrical Circuit-Breaker Box(es):

Location #1 Description: _____
Location #2 Description: _____

Gas Cutoff:

Location #1 Description: _____
Location #2 Description: _____

Pipeline Location:

Location #1 Description: _____
Location #2 Description: _____

Miscellaneous Items:

Car(s): _____

Car Key(s): _____

Hidden key(s): _____

Home Safe: _____

Combination Directions: _____

_____

155

Travel Itinerary

Travel Party: _____ _____ _____

_____ _____ _____

Travel Arrangements:

Frequent Flier Account #: _____   Rewards Club Account #: _____

Travel Dates: _____   Destination(s): _____ _____

Carrier: _____   Flight #: _____   Departure Time: _____

Carrier: _____   Flight #: _____   Departure Time: _____

Carrier: _____   Flight #: _____   Departure Time: _____

Carrier: _____   Flight #: _____   Departure Time: _____

Transportation to Hotel/Resort: **Taxi:** Y / N   **Hotel van:** Y / N   **Rental Car:** Y / N

Transportation to Home: **Taxi:** Y / N   **Hotel van:** Y / N   **Rental Car:** Y / N

Additional parties joining at final destination: _____ _____

Accommodations:

Hotel Name: _____

Address: _____

_____

Phone: _____   Fax: _____

Special instructions/information:

_____

_____

_____

_____

_____

Travel Packing List

Travel Items:

- ❏ Tickets
- ❏ License/Passport
- ❏ Visas
- ❏ Debit/Credit cards
- ❏ Traveler's checks
- ❏ Cash (would suggest to use other forms of payment but this could be helpful for snacks, tips, etc.)
- ❏ Travel Itinerary—two copies; one for you and one left at the house or with friend/relative.

Personal Items:

- ❏ Extra prescriptions
- ❏ Copy of medical history
- ❏ Prescription Medications
- ❏ Glasses/Sunglasses
- ❏ Comb & brush
- ❏ Deodorant
- ❏ Toothbrush & toothpaste
- ❏ Mouthwash
- ❏ Dental Floss
- ❏ Shampoo & conditioner
- ❏ Hair Gel
- ❏ Hairspray
- ❏ Sunblock
- ❏ Nail clippers
- ❏ Tweezers
- ❏ Small sewing kit with needle, thread, buttons, scissors, pins—safety and straight
- ❏ Adapters/converter 110v/220v (if traveling internationally)
- ❏ Hairdryer

Entertainment/Business Items:

- ❏ Ipod/Ipad/Laptop
- ❏ Book/Magazine
- ❏ Cell Phone
- ❏ Business Cards
- ❏ Legal Pad